Journey Beyond Abuse

A Step-by-Step Guide to Facilitating Women's Domestic Abuse Groups

By Kay-Laurel Fischer and Michael F. McGrane

Amherst H. Wilder Foundation
Saint Paul, Minnesota

Manufactured in the United States of America
First printing, August 1997

Edited by Jeanne Engelmann and Vincent Hyman
Designed by Rebecca Andrews

About the Publisher
The Amherst H. Wilder Foundation is one of the largest
and oldest endowed human service and community
development organizations in America. For more than
ninety years, the Wilder Foundation has been providing
health and human services that help children and families
grow strong, the elderly age with dignity, and the community grow in its ability to meet its own needs.

For information about other Wilder Foundation publications, please see the order form on the last page or contact:
Publishing Center, Amherst H. Wilder Foundation,
919 Lafond Avenue, Saint Paul, MN 55104, 1-800-274-6024.

Library of Congress Cataloging-in-Publication Data

Fischer, Kay-Laurel, date.
    Journey beyond abuse : a step-by-step guide to facilitating
women's domestic abuse groups / by Kay-Laurel Fischer and Michael
McGrane.
        p.   cm.
    ISBN 0-940069-14-8
    1. Abused women--Counseling of--Handbooks, manuals, etc.
2. Social work with women--Handbooks, manuals, etc.   3. Social group
work--Handbooks, manuals, etc.   I. McGrane, Michael, date.
II. Title.
HV1444.F57   1997
362.82'9286--dc21   97-34165
                                                                        CIP

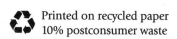

Dedication

Thank you to my friend and partner, John Lindeman, for his belief in gender equality and his consideration of my need for silence in which to write. *KLF*

I would like to thank Gayle, my wife and best friend, for her many years of listening and support. *MFM*

About the Authors

Kay-Laurel Fischer, MA, LP, is a counseling psychologist with the Amherst H. Wilder Foundation Community Assistance Program in St. Paul, Minnesota.

Kay-Laurel coordinates the Women's Domestic Abuse Program at Wilder, provides counseling services for women offenders at Project ReCONNECT, and trains colleagues and other professionals on domestic abuse and group facilitation. She has had a professional focus for over ten years on women's issues and domestic abuse.

Kay-Laurel is a graduate of the Alfred Adler Institute, a licensed psychologist, and a member of Minnesota Women's Psychologists.

Michael F. McGrane, MSW, LICSW, is the director of the Wilder Community Assistance Program. In 1981, Mike founded the Men's Domestic Abuse Program and contributed to the design and implementation of the women's program. He received his master's degree in social work from the University of Minnesota, where he also served thirteen years as a clinical field instructor.

Mike has over twenty-four years of group experience working with perpetrators and victims of abuse. He has trained nationally and internationally. Mike also is the director of Wilder's Youth Violence Prevention Services. He and his colleagues provide direct service, training, and consultation on violence prevention in St. Paul inner city schools.

Mike is a Navy veteran with twenty-six years of active duty and reserve service. He has worked extensively with military and civilian personnel to develop programs for men who batter.

About the Program

The activities in this guide were developed by the staff of the Amherst H. Wilder Foundation Community Assistance Program located in St. Paul, Minnesota. One of the largest such programs in the country, it serves more than six hundred clients each year and provides a comprehensive range of services: prevention, crisis intervention counseling, information and referral, advocacy, culturally specific programming, and assessments for women, men, teens, and children. The Wilder Women's Domestic Abuse Program is one of those services, and the activities and approaches described in this book are all used in that program.

In 1981, Wilder began to develop its services for women who had experienced domestic abuse. The approaches and philosophy in this manual were developed in consultation and collaboration with women's shelters, victims advocates, survivors of domestic abuse, corrections professionals, and practitioners in this and related disciplines. The activities have been refined over many years with the help of many people—most importantly, the women who have participated in our programs.

Other Publications

Over the years, Wilder Community Assistance Program has worked to document its services so others could replicate them and so we could engage in helpful discussion with other people working to change the nature and impact of violence in our country. These publications include:

Foundations for Violence-Free Living: A Step-by-Step Guide to Facilitating Men's Domestic Abuse Groups and the accompanying workbook for participants, *On the Level*. This guide and workbook explain how to provide treatment services for men who batter. The books are published by Amherst H. Wilder Foundation Publishing Center, 919 Lafond Avenue, St. Paul, MN 55104; phone 1-800-274-6024. (See order form in the back of the book for more information on these publications.)

Children's Domestic Abuse Program provides instructions and materials for a twelve-week course for children who have been victims of domestic violence. It is published by Kidsrights, 10100 Park Cedar Drive, Charlotte, NC 28210; phone 1-800-892-5437.

Parenting Under Stress provides instructions and materials for a twelve-session program for parents experiencing stress. It includes sessions on creative parenting, conflict resolution, discipline, nurturing, and child abuse and neglect. It is also available from Kidsrights (see contact information above).

Cool 2B Safe is a series of six videos (plus presenter's and teacher's guides) on violence prevention for use with grades 6-9. It is available from American Guidance Services, 4201 Woodland Road, PO Box 99, Circle Pines, MN 55014; phone 1-800-328-2560.

Acknowledgements

A guidebook such as this can only be written with the gift of *stories* and *experiences* and *tears* from hundreds of women who have been abused. Each of these women contributed something to this book during their journey to living free of violence. Some gave wisdom; some gave compassion; all gave insights as to how abuse impacted their lives. These gifts allowed the Amherst H. Wilder staff, both past and present, to develop a program that has positively affected the lives of women who have been victims of abuse.

In addition to the women themselves, there are several others who deserve recognition for their contributions to this work. A special thanks to Lois Severson for her contributions to the Preface of this book and for her work on behalf of women who have experienced domestic violence. The pioneering efforts of Lois and other advocates to help establish the nation's first shelter for battered women marks a beginning of a journey that continues today.

Many thanks to current Wilder staff members Sheila Craig and Carol Evans for their contributions to the companion journal. Also a heartfelt thank-you to Patti Christensen, a former Wilder staff member, for her seemingly never-ending interest in, support of, and contributions to the curriculum and editing on the manual. A big thank-you is owed to Kathy Tauer for her long keyboard hours and tolerance of author rewrites. Three other contributors to this work are Jeanne Engelmann, Vince Hyman, and Becky Andrews, whose editing, design, and publishing skills brought the work to life.

It should also be noted that although systems and institutional change can be a long and burdensome process, such change is happening in many communities, counties, and states. In Ramsey County, Minnesota, countless strides have been made to address the issue of violence against women. The dedicated efforts of women's shelters, advocates, intervention programs, probation and family court workers, police, judges, child protection staff, and others have been key to providing effective violence intervention and prevention services. It is also important to recognize the efforts of many health care professionals and the progressive work that has been done by Health Partners, a health maintenance organization, in recognizing domestic violence as a health issue. Such work has truly allowed victims of abuse to use services like Wilder's to help break the cycle of violence.

Contents

APPENDICES

Preface

The problem of violence against women remained virtually unrecognized in the United States until the 1970's. At that time, a small group of women who called themselves "volunteer advocates" organized in St. Paul, Minnesota to establish the first battered women's shelter in the nation.

These advocates listened to and believed the stories and recognized the incredible strengths and survival skills of women who came to the shelter. Meeting the basic needs of food, safe shelter, and clothing for the women and children fleeing from their homes became a primary function of the shelter. In addition to meeting these basic needs, the advocates began meeting with women in groups to provide support. For the first time, women had a safe place to express their experience, outrage, and fear without shame or negative consequences. Yet, the advocates' desire to do much more was evident in what followed.

This group of volunteers challenged the status quo and the institutions that failed to protect women from the violence in their homes. Through their efforts, systems changed, laws were written, procedures were enforced, and advocates for women grew in numbers and voice.

One outcome of the work by these advocates can be found in this book. As a response to the advocacy movement, Wilder Foundation started it's women's domestic abuse program to provide support, counseling, education, and advocacy for women in abusive relationships. Since 1981, many women have shared their experiences with other women in the Wilder program. Through this process, they have begun the journey beyond abuse to healing. Wilder has continued to work closely with those who advocate on behalf of women in violent relationships. The work of these courageous women, along with the volunteer advocates, the Wilder Foundation, and many others, has resulted in the group sessions and approaches now documented in this book so that others may duplicate them.

While the violence in our nation's streets brings fear to the hearts of many, we must look behind the closed doors of our homes to uncover the ugly secret of domestic abuse. Violence against women continues to be an enormous problem in this country. Only through the combined and continuous efforts of advocates, shelters, and programs such as the one described here can we begin to make permanent changes in the violence that scars our streets, our homes, and our hearts.

Overview

How to Use the Guidebook

*J*ourney Beyond Abuse is a guidebook for counselors and others who work with or plan to work with women in heterosexual relationships who have been abused by a male partner.[1] It includes a collection of group sessions from our counseling, support, and advocacy experiences with battered women at the Wilder Community Assistance Program in St. Paul, Minnesota. The guidebook describes the process we use and the special issues that typically arise in conducting each of these sessions.

These sessions are the core element involved in helping women understand and heal from the abuse they have experienced. We discuss the underlying philosophy and goals of our program. We describe how we work with women, including initial intake and individual counseling, some recommended practices and policies, and special issues that arise in facilitating these groups. And we provide a set of activities that can be drawn on for your own program. Some of these sessions are essential to our program, and others are optional.

As you use this guidebook please keep in mind the following points.

1. *Read the entire guidebook before using any activities.* The sessions in this guidebook build on each other. It's important that you become familiar with the program's philosophy in order to best facilitate these group sessions and to work with the special issues you may encounter.

2. *This guidebook has three sections:*

   How the Program Works describes the history, philosophy, and goals of this model and how to best use the program. It provides some helpful ideas for conducting individual and group counseling and describes special issues related to domestic abuse group counseling processes with women.

   Group Sessions contains select counseling topics, specific group activities, and activity goals for conducting each session, as well as information about the kinds of issues you may encounter in each group session.

   Appendices contains reproducible forms and other useful materials.

---

[1] *We want to be clear that our work is primarily with women in heterosexual relationships. However, some of these materials can be adapted to work with women involved in same-sex relationships.*

3. *This guidebook is meant to be used with the accompanying participant's journal.* The journal, titled *Moving Beyond Abuse,* is a tool that will help women explore their emotions and thoughts during their participation in the women's program. The questions in the journal enhance the group process. We encourage women to use the journal however they think best. (Note that some women may choose not to write in the journal. This option should be presented to the group and should be respected.)

For some women, writing in a journal is a new activity. Women's responses to journaling will vary, but in our experience this has proven to be a very helpful and well-received tool. We encourage women who find journaling useful to continue it after completion of the group. Instructions for using the participant's journal are on page 20.

4. *This guidebook is set up for ease of use and to help you continuously improve your efforts.* Each activity in the counselor's guidebook includes:

Goals	The goals of the session.
Format	A brief summary of the session.
Activities	Educational content of each group session.
Individual Time Taking	The process and therapeutic component for individual group members.
Closing	The final activity of each group session.
Issues	The important issues that the session raises for both the participants and the counselors.
Notes, comments, and observations	Space to record your observations on the session so that you can adapt and improve it in subsequent presentations.
Worksheets	The actual activity worksheets that can be duplicated and used (collected in the appendices with other reproducible materials).

5. *This guidebook is **only** a guide.* Trust your own instincts and experiences to lead you in this work. There are *many* "right" ways to facilitate women's groups. Every counselor is different and so is every group. What worked well in one group may fall far short in the next. Group dynamics are constantly affecting what happens each week in the group. Your relationship with the group is the *most* significant factor in the group process. At the same time, in spite of your best or worst efforts, the group will find its way.

The facilitator's role is to help guide the process and ensure the physical and emotional safety of all the group members during the group meeting. How you determine to do this may vary greatly, depending on your particular counseling style and presentation. We are simply offering some interventions and methods from which to choose.

We have had a great deal of success with the Wilder model in working with women who have been abused by their male partners. We would also encourage you to adapt and modify the model in ways that best meet the needs of the women you serve.

6. *This program is just a beginning.* Women who have been victims of abuse have survived experiences that are sometimes truly unthinkable and catastrophic. There are no easy answers or simple solutions to address the complex issues of violence against women. In our experience, ongoing processes of support, nurturing, resources, information, and aid in various forms ultimately help meet the woman's individual needs and free her from the violence in her life.

7. *The impact of group work on the group facilitator(s) may require self-care strategies.* Your work as a counselor and group facilitator will place many demands on your own physical and emotional well-being. The stories you will hear, the feelings that will be expressed, and the relationships that will develop are all part of the powerful group experience. It will be important in this process that you pay close attention to yourself and seek out the support you need to carry on with your work.

   There will be moments of doubt, of fear, and possibly of failure. As helpers, we always strive to do our best. We must also know that our best is all we can do. It is easy to be overwhelmed by what we find ourselves faced with as advocates, counselors, helpers, and as human beings concerned for women who have been victimized by their partners. The tragedy of lost dreams and the reality of the lifetime scars women have and will endure sometimes feels like too much to bear. You cannot undo what's been done. Be assured that your work does make a difference. You may never know many of the decisions and changes women will make as a result of the group experience. Just remember that *they* will know.

8. *Many aspects of facilitating a women's domestic abuse program are not covered in this guidebook.* It does not cover specific areas such as funding issues, developing referral sources, marketing, media relations, political and community support, or ways to influence public policy. All of these (and others not listed) are important aspects of running a good program. We assume that you have at least some of these components in place or are working to develop them.

Our hope is that this guidebook will change and grow over time. We welcome your feedback and contributions. We are also available to train or consult with your staff. For questions or comments about any of these activities, contact us at:

Amherst H. Wilder Foundation
Community Assistance Program
650 Marshall Avenue
St. Paul, Minnesota 55104
(612) 221-0048

How the Program Works

This guidebook grows out of years of work by people involved in grass-roots efforts to end violence and abuse, plus a historical examination of these problems and the practical experience of counselors at the Wilder Foundation. In 1981, the Wilder Foundation developed and implemented its domestic abuse programs for both victims and perpetrators of domestic abuse. The counseling services were created in consultation and collaboration with women's shelters, victim advocates, formerly battered women, human service workers, and community corrections personnel. These services are embedded in a larger network of Wilder Foundation services for families and communities.

The model presented in this guidebook is a tested approach. It has been used with more than 1,700 women who have been victims of violence by their male partners. We are confident that this guidebook and the women's journal will provide a valuable resource to counselors of battered or formerly battered women to help them live a life free of violence and abuse.

We believe our model is successful because of the following components:

1. *Our model is based on a combination of teamwork, relationship building, and a philosophy that emphasizes empowerment and support. Teamwork* is expressed through the support that cofacilitators and other staff offer each other in this difficult work. *Relationships* between the facilitators and participants are based on openness, respect, and acceptance. *Empowerment and support* are key objectives in all of the work we do with women; they learn that they are supported in the decisions they make regarding their relationships, their families, and their lives.

2. *We rely on the group process.* In the group, women learn from each other and begin to see how they can support one another in making decisions to be free from violence and oppression in their lives. The group process is essential to a counseling environment that combines respect, support, and understanding. We believe the group members must feel safe. The group process provides support, empathy, resources, and knowledge that leads to empowerment of women in the group.

3. *We use and combine a variety of therapeutic approaches.* These approaches include:
   - A *feminist empowerment* model—understanding the dynamics of abuse, how society sanctions abuse and sexism, and the promotion of egalitarian relationships.
   - A *psychodynamic* model—understanding how the messages we have learned affect our current behavior.
   - An *educational model*—a didactic presentation of material.
   - A *strengths-based* model—understanding one's strengths, capacities, and skills to focus on possibilities and choices.

4. *We firmly believe that initially couples counseling is not effective, prudent, or appropriate when violence has been committed towards a woman by a male partner.* We provide *separate* counseling groups for male perpetrators and battered women. Although the couple may still be in the relationship and request couples counseling, we suggest couples counseling only after each person has received separate domestic abuse counseling. In order for partners to attend couples counseling, the physical abuse must have stopped and the man must not be coercing the woman. We believe relationship issues can only be addressed effectively after the abuse has stopped, after the woman believes she is safe, and after the man has taken responsibility for his abuse.

5. *We recognize that all members of the family system may ask for or need assistance in dealing with the impact of the man's violence.* In practice, we provide groups for male perpetrators, children, parents, and adolescents. While not all agencies can offer this comprehensive list of services, every agency needs to know about and investigate local programs to which they can refer individuals or families for support, advocacy, and other services. (Note, however, that this guidebook only includes group sessions for battered women.)

6. *Our philosophy of abuse comprises eight principles.* We introduce these principles as an activity during the first session, "Eight Program Principles," and discuss them in the description of that activity. The principles are:

   1. Abuse is a learned behavior that has negative consequences for women and children.
   2. Abuse is reinforced by our society.
   3. Abuse can be passed on from generation to generation.
   4. There is no justification for abuse.
   5. Women are not responsible for a partner's abusive behavior, nor can they control a partner's abusive behavior.
   6. Chemical abuse and domestic violence are two separate issues that need to be addressed separately.
   7. Initially, issues of abuse need to be addressed in a setting that is separate and safe from the abusive person.
   8. Each woman has her own answers and timing for addressing issues related to abuse.

7. *We establish high-quality relationships and connections with other community services.* We are connected to a professional community, including women's shelters and children's programs, whose input helps us to continually improve our program and keep in mind the needs of the survivors of domestic violence. We participate on advisory boards and community initiatives, and work closely with other agencies and individuals who serve victims. In addition, our facility is located in or near the communities we serve. We are within reach of other referral sources, families, and neighbors. These connections with our professional and geographical community are vital to maintaining a program that meets the needs of the women.

8. *We employ a flexible, diverse staff.* We feel our program succeeds in part because we select staff who are creative and open to new approaches, able to deal with the diverse cultural backgrounds of participants and other staff, and willing to support one another. These characteristics are especially helpful in reducing staff burnout and turnover.

Using the Activities

There are a total of twenty-one group sessions; some are essential and others are optional. Each session includes goals, group format, session plan and activities, and discussion of issues that may arise. Some sessions include worksheets which can be found in Appendix G. The individual time-taking component of the activities is further described on pages 12–13 of this guidebook.

1. *We recommend having sixteen two-and-one-half-hour group sessions divided into four phases.* The length and number of sessions will vary from program to program. Sixteen weeks is a time frame that allows for the following structure of the group sessions:

   Phase I—Essential Beginnings   6 sessions
   - Introduction to Group
   - Defining Abuse
   - Patterns of Abuse
   - What Keeps Women in Abusive Relationships?
   - Emotional Abuse
   - Anger about Abuse

   Phase II—Most Hurtful Incident   4–5 sessions

   Phase III—Optional Sessions   4–5 sessions
   (Choose according to the needs and
   requests of the particular group)
   - Impact of Negative Messages
   - Common Experiences of Women
   - Impact of Abuse on Children
   - Assertiveness
   - Boundaries
   - Women and Sexuality
   - Questions about Men Who Batter
   - Shame and Guilt
   - Grief and Loss
   - Depression
   - Self-Care
   - Healthy Relationships
   - Evaluating New Relationships

   Phase IV—Closing Session   1 session

Phase I—Essential Beginnings

These six sessions provide a knowledge base about domestic abuse for members of the group. This basic information is important to understanding the dynamics of abuse in general as well as understanding what dynamics are occurring in a particular woman's experience. We highly recommend covering these six Phase I sessions before moving on to other sessions, because future sessions build on this knowledge base.

Phase II—Most Hurtful Incident

The second phase of the sixteen weeks is committed to sessions on each group member's most hurtful incident, or a time for each woman to talk on an individual basis about her feelings of violation due to being abused. The number of weeks this will take depends on the number of women in the group. Usually, two women will share their incident each week. If there are ten women in the group, Phase II will take up to five sessions or weeks. See pages 88–92 for further details on how this phase works.

Phase III—Optional Activities

Phase III is the time when the group members can choose the topics they would most like to learn about for the remaining weeks of the group. As a group facilitator, you could offer any or all of the remaining topics that you are comfortable presenting to be voted on by the group members for the last four or five sessions. Most groups choose *Questions about Men Who Batter*, which you can offer if you have access to a male counselor who has experience working with men who batter. Other popular sessions are *Shame and Guilt*, *Healthy Relationships*, *Assertiveness*, and *Boundaries*.

Phase IV—Closing Session

The final phase of the group is the closing session. This is a most important session and differs in format from all of the others. It is important to plan ahead for this session, as most groups want to include some type of a meal or celebration as part of their good-byes to one another.

A note on clusters: To help you select among the various activities, we have organized them into six clusters as indicated in the table of contents and throughout the session descriptions. We hope these categories will help you as you adapt our program for various lengths, group sizes, cultures, and other unique situations.

2. *The amount of time spent on each of these subject areas can vary from group to group and counselor to counselor.* In each session description there is a suggested time frame; however, this is only a guide. Again, use your counseling style and insights into the group's needs to determine the subjects and length for each session. Feel free to experiment and add or delete material that works for you and your group. Keep in mind that what might have worked well in one group may prove unsuccessful in another. Sometimes you may go into a session planning to discuss one subject but realize that another subject should be discussed, given what is expressed during the group check-in. Adaptability combined with a structured plan provides the needed balance for a successful group session. For more detailed information on the length of sessions, see page 31.

Unique Aspects of Women Participants

Participant Profiles

In a woman's domestic abuse program, you will provide service for voluntary participants and, occasionally, court-ordered participants. *Voluntary* participants are women who have decided on their own, or with the encouragement of another person, to seek services for themselves related to domestic abuse issues. They are usually considered victims or survivors of abuse. *Court-ordered* participants are women who have been ordered by the courts to participate in a domestic abuse program as the perpetrator of the abuse. It has been our experience at Wilder that all of the women who have perpetrated abuse have also been victims of abuse. They may also be seen as a mutual participant in the abusive incident. In some counties, women have been arrested with their partner, which is known as a *mutual abuse* arrest. This issue will be addressed in the Special Issues section of this guidebook. Court-ordered participants are sometimes resistant to attending a domestic abuse group. It will take some special skills and planning to work with voluntary and involuntary participants in the same group.

This guide for women's domestic abuse groups is written for groups that are made up of voluntary participants. No one is demanding that they participate in the group. Consequently, resistance is very rarely an issue that needs to be addressed.

Voluntary participants come for domestic abuse services from a wide variety of referral sources. Some may have little or no knowledge of what the program is about or what it has to offer. Others will have a very good understanding of the program. Clarification of the program and how it works usually occurs during the first phone contact or the initial intake session.

Women who seek counseling or support services are in many different phases of their lives in regard to domestic abuse and their relationships. Some may be currently living with their abuser, and others may have been out of the relationship for a long time. Below are listed some of the possible situations women are in:

- Women who are with their abusive partners and want to stay in the relationship.

- Women who are with their abusive partners and want to make a decision to leave the relationship.

- Women who are with their abusive partners and are unsure of what they want or what is best for them.

- Women who have left the relationship but are unsure of that decision.

- Women who have left the relationship and are being harassed by an ex-partner.

- Women who have left the relationship and no longer have any contact with their ex-partner.

- Women who are in a new relationship and have concerns about abuse beginning to occur again.

- Women who have had multiple abusive partners.

Even though women are frequently in different stages or phases of their abusive relationships, they have many of the same issues and feelings and therefore it is appropriate for them to be in the same group. The common threads of being a victim of abuse and feeling violated are present whether a woman is currently in or out of her abusive relationship.

Inappropriate Participants for Group

On rare occasions, a woman will want to join a group but will not yet be ready for a group or may be inappropriate for other reasons. This can be a difficult but necessary call to make for the well-being of the woman or the group.

Sometimes women will have issues that have affected them in a way that requires some individual counseling to prepare them for the group setting. Or a woman might need more intensive services to address the trauma or abuse she has experienced. There may be some women with mental health issues that require services beyond what the group can offer. These and other potential situations for women who want to join a group are very rare but can occur. It is important for the facilitator to be attuned to this possibility in order to avoid a disservice to any individual woman by including her in a group setting where the expectations are too difficult for her to manage. The facilitator should be aware of available resources that would be appropriate to meet these special needs.

Partners of Group Members

A partner's or ex-partner's behaviors can create unique situations for a woman participating in a domestic abuse group. Women who are still involved with their partner will have different experiences from those who no longer have a partner. Some women will need to "sneak" to the group and hide their participation in the program from their partner. Other women will have a partner who insists that she get help; most of the time his motive is the belief that she "is" or "has" the problem. Some partners will denigrate the group and the woman's right to make changes. Other partners will decide that the problem in their relationship is those "male bashers" and "feminists" from that women's group of hers. Some partners will insist on transporting the woman to and from group in an effort to control what is going on.[2] Others will sabotage a woman's efforts to get to the group at all. It is rare, although it can happen, that a man may sincerely want his partner to get the support she needs and will encourage her to seek help.

Class or Group?

Women may see the domestic abuse group as a class that they attend because they need help. They may feel that they are attending this class because they have done something wrong, in contrast to attending a group because someone has done something wrong to them. Remember women readily shift into taking responsibility for being the "person at fault." In most instances, women are quick to engage as a group and view their experience as a group rather than a class. Others simply think of the group as a class.

---

[2] *We recommend that women not receive rides to group from their partners (see Transportation on page 30) and that partners not be allowed to wait in the building (see Security in the Building on page 47).*

Magical Group Moments

Orchestra conductors talk about moments when performers are so in sync with each other and the composition that they could step down from the podium and the music would continue without direction. The same is true for a women's group. There will be moments when the group is so bonded and in tune with each other that your presence as a facilitator seems unnecessary. You could slip out of the group room and they would barely notice you were gone.

When this occurs, tell the group about it. It gives them a picture of how powerful women can be as a group. It demonstrates a kind of strength and empowerment that they can share with each other to move forward in their journey. It is a moving experience for facilitators as well as group members when a group is self-conducting.

Group Profile

Women in domestic abuse groups are rich in spirit and come together to understand a common problem. Initially, they are often apprehensive and nervous about what may occur in the group. However, at the same time, they may be excited and hopeful about what they may learn from the group.

Groups will look different, act different, and process experiences differently but will almost always come together for a common good. As the group progresses, the group members will be caring, supportive, compassionate, thoughtful, insightful, nurturing, empathetic, and understanding to one another. Group members will change before your eyes as they begin to understand how abuse has affected their lives.

As a facilitator of a women's domestic abuse group, you will likely have an experience that is empowering for you too. You will learn and grow with the participants and gain new tools and skills to continue your work with women.

Is This Group Right for Me?

Typically, one or two women in each group will be unsure if a domestic abuse group is the right group for them. This may happen if a woman has experienced emotional and verbal abuse and has had minimal, if any, physical or sexual abuse in her relationship. Though she may have decided to try the group, she may become even more dubious after a few sessions. She may begin to compare her experience with other group members' experiences and conclude that her situation is "not that bad" and that she might not be appropriate for this group.

As a facilitator, you need to be prepared to address this issue. It can be effective to ask other group members to respond to the women who have doubts. Group peers can usually talk about the futility of comparing abuse and why and how they see a woman's experience as being appropriate for the group. You can also give examples of how feelings are pretty much the same no matter what the abuse is. Being called a degrading name and being punched in the face can cause the same feelings of violation. All violations are hard on self-esteem and self-confidence. Suggest to women in doubt that they reserve judgment on the appropriateness of the group for themselves until after the fourth or fifth session. Be aware that sometimes women are merely looking for reassurance that it is okay for them to be in the group. Also, a woman may not yet have identified the abuse and could actually be unaware of the physical or sexual abuse that occurred in her relationship. This may be identified at a later time in the group process.

Some members may choose to drop out of group. It may not be the right time, it may be too painful, or there may be other reasons. Affirm their decision and invite them to return at some time in the future.

Facilitation Techniques and Standard Group Format

Check-In Process

This is the first activity of every two-and-one-half-hour group session. It is important because it begins each session with a framework that group members can rely on. Each person in the group has a chance to say how she is doing or feeling in a general sense.

The check-in process should be limited to a minute or less per person so that not more than ten to twelve minutes of group time is used. Explain this carefully to group members so that check-in does not become a time to address personal issues at length. Request that the group members and facilitators not ask questions or make comments during check-in. It can often be difficult to refrain as group members will share information with the group that invites questions or comments.

The check-in process can be used in two ways by asking group members to share:

1. A general check-in, such as:
    *   How their week has been
    *   How they are feeling today
    *   How their weekend or holiday went
    *   Whether they would like individual time in the second part of the group

2. A more specific check-in, such as:
    *   How they felt about coming to group today
    *   What they gained from group last week or are getting from group thus far
    *   What they would look like as a weather pattern—sunny, stormy, partly cloudy
    *   High point and low point of the week

Check-in provides a consistent opening for each group and gives each person an opportunity to communicate to the group what she might be feeling or thinking. It also gives a chance to unload an immediate concern that could interfere with listening in group.

Issues that facilitators should be prepared to address are:

- Lengthy check-ins
- A group member in crisis
- Fear of speaking in a group setting
- Emotions that surface unexpectedly

Most of these issues can be addressed by asking if the person can talk about her personal issues after the break, during the **individual time-taking** activity.

Accountability Check-Ins

When there has been a task or an assignment from the preceding week related to any given topic, it is important to have group members report about the assignment. This can usually be done during the check-in of the next group session.

For example, in the assertiveness session, group members are asked to complete an Assertiveness Exercise Worksheet where they will identify a situation and a person with whom they would like to practice an assertiveness skill. The week after the session on assertiveness, ask the group members to comment during check-in on whether they completed the exercise and whether it was helpful for them.

It is important to accept whatever each member's experience was in regard to this assignment. If a woman says she didn't do the exercise, that's okay. If she disliked it, that is okay too. If she completed the assignment and wants to discuss it at length during check-in, this is not okay, and you need to set some limits on her check-in. You might suggest that the report on the assignment be continued during individual time taking.

Individual Time Taking

Individual time taking is the second half of every group session and gives each woman an opportunity to address and process personal issues and concerns. It is the therapeutic part of each group session where appropriate interventions can be made to help a woman better understand how the dynamics of abuse are affecting her.

How does time taking work? In the second half of the group (with sixty to seventy-five minutes remaining), members are asked how many of them would like to talk about a personal issue, concern, or problem that they want to share with the group. This is the time allowed for the group process to work for individual members. It is a time when they can experience validation, symptom relief, encouragement, support, and new insights from their group peers and facilitators. Ask group members to indicate their desire to take time by raising their hand so you know how many women to plan for in the time allotted.

Allow plenty of time for women to decide if they are ready to volunteer for this, as it can be difficult for some women to make this decision. Divide the number of time takers into the available minutes and tell the women how many minutes they each have for their individual use. Hopefully, this will be ten to fifteen minutes per person. Each woman is then given time to say what she wants to the group without interruption. When she is finished, she is asked if she would like responses from the group members and facilitators. This is generally referred to as feedback. Most women are open and anxious to get feedback from their peers.

Feedback comes in many forms—some appropriate and some less appropriate— and usually needs to be guided by the group facilitator. Appropriate feedback is caring, empathetic, encouraging, insightful, validating, clarifying, a sharing of information, a reporting of observations, and is time-limited and precise. Not all feedback in a group is appropriate. Examples of less appropriate feedback include giving advice, asking "why" questions, wanting to fix the problem, not staying on the issues the time taker has presented, judging, blaming, or rambling on about one's own experience that might be similar.

You will need to coach group members in how to give appropriate feedback if they lack these skills. Usually though, most group members have a good sense of how to be appropriate with feedback. Most often they understand about talking one at a time and not monopolizing more than their share of the time.

Keeping the time takers on schedule can be difficult. The ten to fifteen minutes go by very rapidly for the person presenting the issue and for the group feedback. Group facilitators need to make certain that each member gets the time that was allowed for her. The group facilitators must have a watch and be ready to give verbal notice of minutes remaining. Sometimes a group member must be interrupted and gently told that the group must move on to the next person. At other times group members are willing to give up their allotted time to a person who needs extra time. This is acceptable as long as it is volunteered. In rare circumstances, a member can be asked to give up her promised time, if, for example, a group member begins to experience flashbacks or post-traumatic stress. There are situations that clearly need additional processing time.

The ideal closure for each time-taking individual is to tell the woman who is taking time that she will have the last word and ask her how she feels after receiving the group feedback. Remember to remind women that they are not obligated to use any feedback that doesn't work or feel right for them.

Feelings

Women's groups are often about feelings. In the group, members are looking to acknowledge feelings, identify feelings, express feelings, get support for feelings, and be less ashamed of their feelings. Sometimes this is an overwhelming task, as it is difficult to move that great distance from head to heart to find the feelings.

It is a good idea for facilitators to have a copy of the Feelings Vocabulary sheet (Appendix C) ready to use at any time during this group. When a woman cannot identify a feeling, you can offer her the Feelings Vocabulary list to assist her in the identification process. This can be very helpful to women in the group as it reduces the stress related to thinking of a particular feeling on their own.

Unfocused Participants

On occasion, there will be a group member who has a difficult time staying focused or on task. This person can present in many different ways and sometimes needs an intervention by the facilitator that will help the member adjust to the group process. Groups are not necessarily a natural setting for everyone. Learning to participate in a group may take some assertive coaching by the facilitators.

Some examples of how such a participant may present herself in group include: frequently interrupting others who are speaking; having input on every topic; always needing to be the first to speak; being consumed with her thoughts and constantly needing to express those thoughts; wanting individual time taking every week; wandering off in her thoughts somewhere into a place by herself; or telling every detail of every situation beyond what is needed to make her point.

However the unfocused participant presents, it is your job as the facilitator to recognize whether this lack of focus represents a problem for the group or the woman and to address the problem with an appropriate intervention. This can be difficult with some members, but is best done from your sense of care and concern.

There are many appropriate interventions, and your tone of voice is extremely important to your success. Careful timing is important as well. Successful interventions may include:

- Asking a woman to "hold onto her thoughts" for a few moments until you can get to her.
- Asking if other women in the group, besides the woman who is speaking, have any feedback or response.
- Expressing to a woman what your honest feelings, as the facilitator, are when she is unfocused and rambling.
- Asking the group members if they have any response or feedback for a given situation with an unfocused member.
- Referring to the group expectations or rules that are pertinent to the situation.
- Stating that you want every group member to have an opportunity to use the group time fairly.
- Helping a woman to summarize what she is saying so she can better express the point she wants to make.

The unfocused participant can be difficult for you and the group or may simply be a participant who needs more support from you as the group facilitator. Each unfocused participant is unique and often needs special care and attention from you and the group to participate appropriately and to feel as if she belongs. Sometimes a participant who displays this kind of behavior can be easily scapegoated by the group. The group may become frustrated or angry and may possibly ignore or isolate her. The facilitators may also want to check what verbal and nonverbal messages they are giving to the group related to the unfocused or difficult-to-manage participant.

Fearful and Shy Participants

Some group members are so shy or fearful of the group that it will take extra care and delicate interventions to help them become actively involved in the group process. It usually works well to respect their right to just observe, listen, and pass for a few group sessions while they are integrating what is going on around them. Sometimes it can be helpful if one of the facilitators sits next to the shy or fearful individual. This positioning may give the participant a sense of security during the first or second meetings.

After a period of time, the facilitator could gently ask for the opinion or any comments from anyone who has remained silent. The facilitators can state something along the lines of "I know you have thoughts on what we're discussing; the group loses out if we don't get to hear from you."

Usually, fearful and shy group members are glad to be encouraged to express themselves. They often have wonderful things to say and just need some help in finding a space and time to say what they are thinking. After being encouraged to have an equal voice in the group a few times, most fearful and shy participants will find a comfort level and will participate on their own from then on. Only a very few women will need a facilitator's support and encouragement throughout the group process.

Emotionally Overwhelmed Participants

Some women come into the group overwhelmed by their feelings of sadness, despair, or hurt. They may cry through much of the group process and often are unable to speak because they can't talk without crying. It is not uncommon for such a group member to feel embarrassed and like a spectacle in the group.

It is usually appropriate to acknowledge this group member's feelings. When the timing is right, you can ask her if she'd like to talk about what is going on for her. She may or may not want to speak about her feelings.

Some women seem to just want to be left alone to do some grieving in the group in a silent manner. Others may want to be encouraged to state what is occurring for them. Some may even want to take their feelings of sadness to feelings of anger. It is important for facilitators to be sensitive to what the participant who is feeling emotional might need. Women in the group generally will be supportive of this person, whether she expresses herself or not.

There are also times when a woman may need to leave the group room. The facilitators can offer this option to the group ahead of time. Because it can be disruptive to the rest of the group when a member leaves, plan ahead to handle this. For example, a facilitator, cofacilitator, or another group member can plan to check on the group member shortly after she leaves the room.

Advice Giving

Advice giving is almost always unhelpful and discounting for a woman. She usually has her own answers and only needs support to make new choices. You can, however, help a woman explore her options regarding her situation. This process may help her determine how to best meet her needs and be safe. It is also common for group members to ask other members for advice. The facilitators will need to help the group handle advice-seeking.

This can be one of the most difficult practices that the facilitator may encounter. Experience has told us time and time again that *information and support is powerful; advice is not.* Often a woman will comment later in the process how much she appreciated that the facilitator let her make her own decisions. Women often will comment on how well the counselor listened and heard what they had to say.

It is extremely difficult for counselors and advocates who are keenly aware of the dangers that face battered women not to encourage a strong and immediate response that says, "Get away from the abuser, press legal action, get safe, or end the relationship now." Our philosophy is to provide support, advocacy, and information to the women we serve to help empower them to make their own decisions in their own time. This includes using everything in our power—the facilitator, the group, the courts, shelters, and agency and community resources—to provide women with choices to help them become safe from the violence in their lives.

As counselors, advocates, therapists, or others providing services to battered women, we often find it extremely difficult to hold our opinions or advice to ourselves. This is especially true when we have so much statistical and anecdotal data that supports our beliefs. We should not ignore these beliefs, facts, or experiences. *Our experience is that what helps to empower the women we have served is knowledge and truth—not opinions and advice.* Sometimes it's a fine line—one that we can only encourage you to think about and then proceed with *your* best thinking on this issue.

Validation Technique

The following technique can be used artfully and successfully to reduce shame and to validate a woman's feelings. Ask each member of the group to respond to something that a particular group member has said.

For example: A group member is talking about her abusive situation and begins to cry and states that she feels "so stupid" for ever marrying her husband. You could gently intervene and ask her if she would like to hear what the group's opinion is on what she just said. Usually the woman will agree to this. State that you will go around the circle and have each person in the group respond to what she has just said. You can ask the person next to her to begin by commenting briefly on whether the woman was stupid for marrying her husband. Then continue around the circle so that each person gets a chance to respond to her.

As a whole, women are very supportive and understanding and will give great feedback and encouragement to someone who is feeling ashamed. Most women will directly state that the person is not stupid and will expand on why they think that. It can be validating and shame-reducing to have several voices express why a woman's thoughts shouldn't have to be so painful and difficult for her. It can be moving to watch this process occur. After going around the group, ask the woman who has been given the feedback for her final thoughts and feelings.

There is always the potential for someone to give shaming feedback or to launch into her own story or thoughts. As a group facilitator, you need to help this person move on and undo any damage that may have been done by diffusing or restructuring what might have been said.

Talking about Men

Not a single group session will go by without the issue of men coming to the surface. This may seem to be an obvious point when we are talking about heterosexual females who have been or are involved with male partners. What may not be so obvious is how the conversations, comments, or discussions may occur during the group sessions and what the role of the facilitators is when the issues and descriptions are discussed in group.

Women who have been abused by their intimate male partners can feel a great deal of anger, hurt, anguish, revenge, and many other strong emotions. Feelings such as love, hope, confusion, or fear may be just as strong. For example:

First woman: "I love my husband and I know he loves me. He's a good provider and father and most of the time he's not abusive. If he only could learn to be that way all the time, everything would be fine . . . "

Second woman: "I gave that rotten bastard fifteen years of my life and this is all I've got to show for it—nothing but physical and emotional scars that have messed me up for a lifetime. I don't even want to see a man again. They're all the same— worthless jerks who should be locked up forever . . . "

When these feelings come out in group, they tend to come with such passion and spontaneity that they can take the group and facilitator by surprise. In the above example, two group members are in very different places with their thoughts, feelings, and experiences. The question is, what is the impact on each of these women and the rest of the women when these strong statements are made in group? How does the group facilitator respond?

As facilitators, we know that each woman in the group is in a different place in her relationship. Each woman also becomes very aware of how she fits in with other women in the group. Therefore, it is very important to establish some group expectations at the beginning of the group that can be referred to when these differences begin to arise (see Group Expectations, pages 57-58). The most important expectation is to respect each woman and not impose personal values or feelings on others—to unconditionally accept each other and allow each woman to feel respected and accepted for her own position and process.

Our approach to talking about men in group is to not make judgmental, categorical, or generalized statements that depict all men or some men in any particular way. Male bashing, stereotyping, and other negative or destructive comments about men are inappropriate and unproductive. Although there are certainly times when a group member may make such comments in a moment of anger or disgust, it is important that the group facilitator help the group members focus on the feelings or the issues.

Women who have been abused have every right to their feelings towards their abuser. Minimizing male bashing in group is not meant to stifle the women's feelings or protect the abuser. It does imply cultivating respect toward the other group members who may feel differently and do not want to hear stereotyping or male bashing comments. Avoiding this kind of talk also respects the fact that not all men are abusive towards women and should not be categorically lumped by gender into this position.

Handouts

There are hundreds of pieces of literature, information, and poems that are appropriate and can be used as handouts in a women's domestic abuse group. You'll need to make your own decisions about how many and how often handouts will be used.

- Things to be considered when deciding about the use of handouts are:
- Is the handout appropriate and helpful to the particular session?
- Are copyright laws being respected regarding any use of materials?
- What is a good limit on the number of handouts?
- How should the handout be used? (Will it be read during the group, given out at the end of group to take home, or used as the closing for a given session?)

Group members often like handouts that have some particular meaning or something that gently touches them. They also like handouts that relate to the information covered in a given session; it seems to be helpful to reinforce the information this way.

Another source of handouts is chalkboard notes generated from the group itself. A cofacilitator or group member records the information being presented and written on the chalkboard for any given session; it is then typed, copied, and distributed as a handout the following week. This type of handout is helpful because the information is personalized to the group.

Whatever the bias on handouts, it is important to avoid overwhelming group members with too much information all at once. It may be wise to limit the number of handouts, particularly at the beginning stages of a group.

If possible, provide folders at the first session so group members have a place to keep the handouts.

Weekly Closing

This final activity of every group session gives closure and allows each group member an opportunity to say something in the group.

The closing should be limited to the last five minutes of group. Comments and questions are usually not appropriate during closing. Again, this can be difficult for some members, so it should be carefully explained in advance. Facilitators also participate in the closing process.

The closing can be conducted in a number of ways. Ask each member to:

- Describe how she feels in one word.
- Name one thing learned from group which she can take away with her.
- Ask participants to share one strength or positive comment about herself with the group ("I am *wise*").
- Ask participants to tell the person to their right a positive trait or strength they see in that person.
- Ask participants to set a short-term goal to work on in the next week.

These are only a few examples of possible closings to be used at the end of group. Facilitators can be creative in thinking of ideas for this process. Group members can also be asked for their ideas. The important thing is to keep it simple and brief. If a woman has difficulty responding to the closing exercise, ask her if she'd like to pass for the moment, then tell her you will come back to her at the end.

Preparing Groups for Final Closure

The process of closure in a women's group is very important. Over the period of several months, women generally become very attached and bonded to each other. The thought of the group coming to a close can be disturbing and even frightening for some. Group members have often come to depend on the weekly meeting for support and good feelings and do not look forward to it ending. Thus, the closing process becomes an important part of the group.

Our recommendation is to begin closure for the group about three to four sessions before the end. You might ask during check-in or closing how it feels to have only a few group sessions remaining. Keep comments brief at this time. Be aware that some members are ready for the group to end. However, many members will not be ready and will talk about wishing the group could last longer. All feelings are appropriate and can be validated.

Allow group members to discuss the end of the group for a few weeks before the last session. This begins to set the tone for the final phase of the group. The last session focuses mainly on the closure process. This is the time when each group member is given an opportunity at greater length to communicate feelings about the group coming to an end. See the Closing Session on page 164.

Using the Guided Journal

Moving Beyond Abuse: Stories and Question for Women Who Have Lived with Abuse is a separate book and complements the sessions in this guidebook. It is a journal for the women to purchase and keep, where they can write their personal thoughts on topics related to abuse and their own experience.

The journal is intended to:

- Reinforce what is learned in the group
- Help women further explore their thoughts on any individual topic related to abuse
- Encourage future writing as a way to address personal issues, ideas, thoughts, and feelings
- Experience the stories of other women who have been abused

Each topic covered in the guidebook has a complementary activity in the journal. The statements, ideas, and questions directly relate to what is covered in the activity corresponding to that topic.

Since not all topics will be covered in the group over the sixteen weeks, some journal sections will be foreign to the woman using them. Each woman can decide on her own if she cares to write in the sections that were not covered in group. This should be explained when the journals are distributed, to clarify any potential confusion.

Another issue related to the journal is safety. Some women are fearful of keeping the journal in their own homes and of finding a safe place for it where people in their lives will not violate their privacy. Talk about this in the group so that each member will consider what is best for her.

If a woman decides she cannot feel safe with her journal in her possession, facilitators can offer to keep it for her during the course of group. Of course, this would mean she would have to come to the group location to do her writing. This may be logistically difficult but can be accomplished before or after the group session.

It is extremely important that each woman think about what is best for her on this matter. It may be wise to encourage her to err on the side of safety. She knows best what the repercussions might be if someone invaded her private thoughts and space.

Journals are available from the Wilder Publishing Center, 919 LaFond Avenue, St. Paul, MN 55104, toll-free 1-800-274-6024. There is an order form at the end of this book.

Intake and Individual Counseling

Initial Phone Contact

Generally, the initial contact by a woman for domestic abuse services is a phone call. This call may be very difficult for a woman to make, and the person taking the initial call should be trained on how to respond (see First Contact with the Agency, on page 27). The woman could then be referred to the phone intake counselor or asked to leave her name and number and a good time for a call to be returned to her. For more information about handling phone calls to the participant, see Returning Calls to Participants, on page 28.

Initial Counselor Intake Call

The next step is for the counselor who does the telephone intake to talk to the prospective participant. When returning the call, ask if this is a good time for the woman to talk. This phone conversation is a time to establish whether or not the available services are appropriate for her. Before presenting the overview of the program, find out who referred her to your agency. Then briefly cover the following information:

- Overview of the services
- Type of group
- Length of group
- Starting date of the next group
- Day and time
- Location
- Cost of group

After this description, ask the woman if this sounds like what she is looking for and if she has any questions. Usually she will want to know about the cost of the program. Be prepared to discuss your program's fees. Do you take insurance, have a sliding or reduced fee, have outside funding or scholarships? Will you help women find funding to cover the program cost? Can you apply for crime victim funding? After a payment method has been explored and established, questions have been answered, and the woman has indicated her interest in your services, communicate the next steps for pursuing membership in this group.

Tell her that you need to get a little information from her now over the phone. (See next page for a summary of suggested information you may want during this initial contact.) After getting whatever information is needed for your program, let her know that the next step is to arrange an intake session with the person who will be facilitating the group. Tell her that the counselor will contact her directly to set up the intake appointment. Communicate that once the intake session is completed, she is ready to begin the group. All of this, of course, assumes that an individual intake will be done before the start of a group. If this is not your program's policy, tailor this section to your procedures.

If the woman chooses to proceed, you might want to ask her for the following information:

- Name
- Address
- Date of birth
- Home phone
- Work phone
- Best time of day to contact
- Precautions in contacting her
- Referral source
- Payment method

- Name of abusive partner
- Relationship status
- Miscellaneous information

Also note:

- Date
- Phone intake person
- Group assignment
- Group facilitator

Tell her the name of the person who will call her for the intake session and approximately when she can expect the call. Tell her she is welcome to call you back if she has any more questions or needs to talk before the intake.

Once the participant's interest is established and the payment method is in place, the group facilitator calls to set up the intake session. Sometimes finding a time slot that can be agreed upon by both parties is difficult. It is nice if you can be flexible with sessions that are early or late in the day, or over a lunch hour to accommodate working women.

Intake Session

You have now arrived at the next step, the face-to-face intake session. Ideally, this meeting is held in a private space that is comfortable and feels safe. Introduce yourself to the new prospective group member and ask her to join you in the designated area. Offer coffee or water if possible and lead the way to the office. When you arrive at the door of the office, allow her to enter first and communicate that she can sit wherever it looks comfortable to her.

Begin the session with what feels comfortable to you. You might ask if she had any trouble finding the location, if she would like to remove her coat, comment on the weather, and so on. If you have business cards, give her one and write the starting date and time of the group on the back of it.

Next, tell her what you will be doing in the intake session and what you hope to accomplish. Tell her that after the paperwork has been completed to establish her as a participant with your program, there will be plenty of time to talk about her individual situation. Communicate that you will be doing an evaluation about the abuse so that both of you have a picture of what she has experienced. Mention that, at the end of this session, you want to set a few goals with her for what she wants out of the group. Ask if she has any questions before you begin.

If the participant looks very uncomfortable or scared, ask if there is anything you can do to help alleviate her fears. Depending upon what the woman offers as her concerns, you may need to spend time on the issues she's presenting and delay moving forward with the intake process. Once you feel comfortable moving on, proceed with the needed paperwork for your program or agency. Talk about and sign any needed release forms. Communicate participant rights and responsibilities and client privacy. Try to accomplish all of the above within ten minutes unless there are serious issues that prevent you from moving forward. Try to keep the participant focused on this until it's completed.

Next, suggest that you do the evaluation of her abuse (Appendix D, page 173)[3]. Ask if she can get comfortable in her chair and give her a copy of the scale to be used for her answers. Hand her a sheet of paper with the following on it:

1 = Never   4 = Often

2 = Rarely   5 = All the time

3 = Sometimes

Remind her that this is being done for both you as the counselor and her as the participant so that each of you will have a better picture of what her experience has been. Read the instructions (Appendix D) and proceed by asking:

How often has your partner:

a) Yelled at you

b) Refused to talk to you

c) And so on (see page 173 for a complete list of questions)

Allow the participant plenty of time to think of her response and do not rush her. When the questionnaire has been completed, ask the participant how it felt to respond to these questions. Give her time to understand and integrate how powerful it can be to name and acknowledge abuse. Show her the form and point out the pattern that appears. Communicate to her the types of abuse (physical, verbal, sexual, emotional) that appear to be a part of her experience.

Next, tell her you want to do an open-ended questionnaire that will give her an opportunity to talk about her situation. Use Appendix E, page 175 for this part of the intake. This should take ten to fifteen minutes to cover, plus additional time if the participant has a need to express more details on the situation.

Finally, talk about setting goals that she wants to work on in the group (Appendix F, page 179). Offer suggestions if she has difficulty with these, and try to have a general discussion about possible goals. After this is completed, ask her about what she sees as her strengths. Again, help her see a few if identifying them is too difficult for her.

It is helpful to have a list of local women's resources to give her as she leaves (intervention programs, women's shelter numbers, victim's hot lines). Suggest she share it with someone else if she doesn't need it. Ask her how she felt about the intake session and how she feels about coming into the group. Tell her you will contact her the week of group to remind her again of the starting date. Also mention that she is welcome to contact you about any questions or concerns.

---

[3] *This evaluation is adapted from materials developed by Murray A. Straus at The University of New Hampshire, Durham. Used with permission.*

Individual Counseling Sessions

From time to time participants will request individual counseling in conjunction with the group. Consider what your policy and capacity for this will be. The requests for individual counseling could be made at the initial intake session, during the course of group, or after the group is over. The following are suggestions on how you might address these requests.

When a woman asks for individual counseling sessions at the intake session, consider what the need is at that time. Sometimes a woman is in crisis and needs additional services. Sometimes the starting date of the group is several weeks or more in the future, and a woman clearly needs support until the group begins. A few individual sessions may be a way of meeting these needs, and this option might be considered as a part of your program's policy.

When the group is in progress, some women will want individual sessions in addition to the group. This may or may not be appropriate, depending on the circumstances of each woman and your program's resources. Some women need an individual session or two to strengthen their courage to address issues in the group. Some women may have too many issues to address in group and need additional time so as not to use too much of the group time. Other women may want additional attention from you and feel they're not getting enough out of the group. There will be many reasons that women request individual sessions, and women who are being abused often have many issues for which they may seek additional support. Your job is to decide what your capacity or practice is regarding individual counseling that is requested in addition to the group.

It is not uncommon to get calls from women after groups have ended requesting individual counseling. This can happen anywhere from weeks to years after the group is over. Again, what is important is that you are not caught off guard and know how you want to address this request. One idea is to see the woman for one or two sessions to assess her needs and refer her to an appropriate counseling setting. Another idea is to suggest on the phone that she begin attending an ongoing support group for women in the community, in a women's shelter, or in your program (if one has been developed for continuing care). Sometimes women only need to see you individually for one or two sessions to receive confirmation on what they are thinking and planning to do. Most women will feel safe and comfortable calling their counselors when issues arise. It is important to plan a response in advance that will establish the realistic limits and resources of your program and staff. Because this is not always easy to do, advance planning can help both the participants and the program staff.

Recommended Policies and Practices

Every program has its own unique policies, practices, and data collection requirements. Local and state regulations and state professional codes of conduct also influence policies. We recommend that you develop policies or releases to deal with the following issues:

Tennessen Warning

The following is an abbreviated sample of the Tennessen Warning issued to participants who provide initial information over the telephone:

"Before I can ask you to give me any information I must explain who can see it and how it will be used. The information you give will be used by the staff of this agency to help you determine the kind of service or assistance you need. No law requires that you give us information, but we cannot help you without some information. What you say will be kept private, but it could be reviewed by officials who work in the programs you participate in.

"If you are a minor, you can ask that data about you be kept from your parents."

Participant Rights and Responsibilities

We ask each participant to read and sign a sheet explaining her rights as a participant and what we expect of her. She can expect the right to:

- Respectful and courteous service.
- Information on her assessment, recommended counseling, and estimated length of service.
- Explanations of all releases, requirements, and fees.
- Refuse treatment or choose to receive counseling elsewhere, within the limits imposed by insurance coverage or court order.
- Information about other services available in the community.
- Coordinated transfers to other service providers if needed.
- Advance notice of changes in service or fees.
- Assert these rights without retaliation.
- Discuss with the counselor his or her training.

Some of the participant's responsibilities include the responsibility to:

- Be respectful of staff and others.
- Be on time or call in advance to reschedule.
- Not come for services under the influence of alcohol or other mood-altering substance.
- Follow smoking ordinances.
- Pay fees (when applicable).

Data Privacy and Confidentiality

This is a crucial area for participants. In most states, mandatory reporting laws allow certain records to be subpoenaed. Be sure to:

- Discuss who you must inform and what you must do if you hear about child abuse or neglect or if you believe the participant is going to hurt herself or someone else. Explain any state or local laws.

- Explain how you communicate with court officials and to what extent you share information. Be sure your information releases clearly explain the nature of your contact with officials and what information is usually exchanged.

- Explain how the program responds to court subpoenas ordering the program to turn over case notes or information regarding the participants.

- If you are doing any program evaluation related to the information that participants give you, ask their permission and explain the nature, use, and availability of the research to others.

- Explain what information will be available to the participant from your records, whether you will be writing any summary reports, and to whom you will send these reports.

Releases of Information

Information releases are needed for you to speak to anyone outside of your program about the participant. This could include court workers, ex-partners, relatives, and others. At intake or individual counseling sessions, explain when these are needed and when they are not needed for you to share information. In particular, discuss who you need releases from—for example, the participant's physician, psychologist, social worker, shelter personnel, and other programs she is participating in that request information from you.

It is rare that women refuse to sign the release forms. However, a woman may be extremely hesitant to sign, based upon her previous history or experiences with individuals or systems. It is important to discuss these concerns with her and determine what course of action to take. It should be made clear to her that some of the reporting requirements are governed by law and are nonnegotiable. Usually further explanation of the forms and addressing her concerns will satisfy most questions.

Use of Alcohol and Other Mood-Altering Drugs

We strongly recommend that you develop a policy that prohibits attending the group while under the influence of alcohol or other mood-altering drugs. Explain this policy to each participant and ask if she feels she can abide by this expectation. Explain that attendance in group while under the influence of chemicals prevents her from learning and distracts other members of the group. Explain the consequences for this behavior and that the final determination of her condition will be in your hands. The approach we usually use is to ask a woman who is using chemicals to leave the group and to contact her counselor the next day to talk about what must take place for her to reenter the group.

Living with Her Abuser

Our program philosophy is to unconditionally accept a woman's decision of whether or not she stays with her abusive partner or has contact with him. We do not give her advice on this matter or imply what would be best for her. As it applies, we do share concerns for her safety. We will assist her in exploring her options and provide resources that may help her with her decision on this issue. (See page 45 for safety plan information.)

Special Issues

There are countless issues that arise at various times during a woman's involvement in the domestic abuse program. These issues can be identified from the initial phone call to years after the woman has participated in the program. While no book could include all the issues that arise, we offer information on the following topics:

- First Contact with the Agency
- Returning Calls to Participants
- Child Care
- Transportation
- First Week of Group
- Size of Group
- Length of Sessions
- Open- versus Closed-ended Groups
- Group Setting
- Support versus Therapy
- Facilitator Teams
- Group Members Who Know Each Other
- Group Members and Staff Who Know Each Other
- Groups Not Bonding

- Attrition
- Group Is Not for Everyone
- Power of the Group Experience
- Using Inclusive Language
- Special Needs
- Substance Abuse
- Societal Myths and Messages
- Women Who Have Perpetuated Abuse
- Putting One's Hope in Treatment of the Abusive Partner
- Safety and Protection
- Group Phone Lists
- Use of Video and Films
- Security in the Building
- Mutual Arrest

First Contact with the Agency

What information must the support staff know about a potential participant who calls the agency?

The support staff should be trained by the experienced counseling staff who are conducting the services for the women's program. This training should focus primarily on the support staff's role and responsibilities as these pertain to best serving the potential participants who call the program.

Counselors should emphasize how important the support staff's role might be in that first contact with the group member. Establishing a clear and consistent procedure will help the support staff know exactly how to direct or answer the caller's initial questions. One effective training method is to provide role-play situations that would accurately reflect the real-life situations of your program's *initial contact* experiences. Ongoing dialogue and training for staff who are in these unique and essential roles is important.

Sometimes when women make that initial call they are in a state of crisis or are unsure how or what they want to ask the support staff. The support staff's training should provide adequate skills and information to effectively address the caller's questions and refer her to the designated counseling staff.

It is critical that the support staff understand what the woman caller might be experiencing. For example, it may have taken the woman several months or years to make this call. Or possibly the woman has just been beaten up by her abuser. The support staff members are *not* expected to be counselors, but are expected to address the woman in a caring, calming voice when giving her the program information.

Depending on the program's staffing and practice, this initial contact could come in different forms (phone, in person, and so on) and may also involve various staff. The key is to recognize the importance of this initial contact with the victim. It could make the difference between providing her with hope and resources or possibly contributing to further victimization or a sense of hopelessness.

Returning Calls to Participants

We address this because of the extreme importance of participants' safety. The best way for you to know how to be protective toward participants and prospective participants is to ask them during initial contact how future calls to them should be handled.

Ask if it is okay to leave messages for them with others who might answer at home or at work numbers. Inquire about how to handle messages on voice-mail or answering machines. Whatever the participant tells you she wants regarding return calls, make a note of it so you will have the information at hand when you return a call to her.

Child Care

Access to child care is one barrier to getting counseling services. Women who seek help and support for themselves to escape the violence in their lives do not forget the safety needs of their children. Many women who may want support or counseling services are in very difficult and unique positions.

One issue may be affordability of child care. Women in abusive relationships sometimes have limited or no financial resources. If the woman does have money, it may be monitored or controlled by her abuser; therefore, asking for money for child care may expose her attempt to get help, making it difficult or impossible for her to leave. She may also be isolated from family or friends, making it difficult to find someone to provide consistent, short-term care.

A major fear is leaving her children in the care of the abuser. A woman's partner may have abused the children in the past. She may fear that he might use this time to abuse, emotionally manipulate, or interrogate the children in her absence. If she decided to leave the children with her abusive partner, it might be difficult for her to focus on her own needs during the group sessions. She could be preoccupied with the situation her children were in and worry about the possible outcomes.

At Wilder we are able to provide free child care (within limits) for the women who attend groups. Child care is conducted in the same facility using experienced and competent adult staff. There is one night during the week when the sixteen-week women's groups, the women's aftercare support group, and the child care are offered at the Wilder site. All other Wilder participant groups (men's, children's, adolescent's, and others) are held on other days and times. This provides a safe and secure time and place for women and their children to have their own space.

The focus of child care is on play, creative expression, and positive interaction with the other children and adults. There is no formal counseling or therapy provided for the children during this time. However, informal work such as listening to the children talk about their day at school or home happens in this setting. A light, healthy snack is also provided.

When some children start in child care, they become anxious and may not want to detach from their mother. This situation is understandable for many children, and even more so for children who have lived in abusive homes.

The child-care staff have many creative interventions which, in most cases, immediately help the child feel comfortable and begin to participate in the play activities. The child-care staff also try to work with the mothers to solicit their ideas and gather important information about the child that may help the child through the initial crisis. Almost without exception, the children (even the children experiencing a high level of separation anxiety) enjoy and look forward to coming to child care. They feel safe and welcomed, and they have fun.

It may not be possible to provide child-care services for the women who attend your program. Keep in mind that without available child care, some women will not be able to receive services. They will place their children's needs over their own. Complex child-care arrangements may also affect a woman's attendance in the group and possibly affect her likelihood of completing the group. On the other hand, the women we serve are very resourceful and have found many ways to meet their children's needs as well as their own.

Transportation

A second critical barrier for women having access to group services is transportation. Again, some women have limited resources and limited access to transportation. Unfortunately, as with child care, there are no easy answers to this issue. Getting her children and herself ready for a long bus ride at the end of a stressful day is not easy.

For some women it's not only an issue of access to a car, bus, or cab; it also may be an issue of disclosure. She may not want her partner (or others) to know where she is going. In the case of having to depend on her abusive partner for transportation to group, this could be problematic and even dangerous. If at all possible, we suggest that women not depend on getting rides to or from the group with their abusive partner. There are many control and safety problems that can occur when they are with him.

Often when women leave the group sessions, they have been deeply affected by what was shared and discussed. It is best if each woman has some time by herself with her thoughts and feelings, if possible, rather than having to share them with her abusive partner.

Sometimes other women in the group may offer ideas on how to help resolve transportation problems. There are times when women will offer rides to other members of the group. This option can work but may present other problems. For example, if the woman who is the driver cannot make it to group, the other riders may also be unable to come. There are times when these arrangements between group members can cause hard feelings or difficulties that could affect the group process. Although for the most part these situations are productive and go without issue, it is important to be aware of potential problems and of ways to prevent them from occurring.

Finally, there may be some resources available (grant moneys, a charitable agency, and so forth) to fund transportation requests in part or whole.

First Week of Group

It is helpful to make contact with every group member the week that the group begins. It is possible, depending on when the intake was held, that you will not have spoken with some group members for several weeks.

This preliminary contact allows you to remind each woman of the starting date and time of the group and to address any questions or apprehension she may be feeling about the group. If a woman expresses fear or doubt about the group at this time, it is important to give her an opportunity to talk about her concerns. You can assure her that the feelings are not uncommon and that you will make every effort to help her become comfortable with the group. You may want to encourage her to at least attend the first group session and then make a more informed decision about whether or not she would like to continue.

It is also helpful to request that all group members arrive ten to fifteen minutes early for the first session so that you can begin the first session on time.

Size of Group

The size of a women's domestic abuse group varies depending on whether there are one or two facilitators. Our experience is that a group with eight to ten members works well with one facilitator and ten to twelve members with two facilitators. Twelve members is a large group, but it can work well, particularly if both facilitators are experienced. Any number over twelve is cumbersome for this type of group and will be less effective when addressing individual therapeutic issues. Any number less than eight is usually too small; when absences and expected attrition are considered, a number less than eight has too much potential for becoming a size that is neither effective nor therapeutic. It is important to note, though, that there really is not a magic or correct group size. It is possible to have a group of four or five members who will have as powerful a therapeutic experience as a larger group.

One of the ways to have more control over group size is to be willing to take in new members through the second session of a group. This is our policy at Wilder, and it has worked very well. This way, if you lose a member or two after the first session, you can add new members at the second session to achieve the desired number. To create a cohesive and safe group, do not add new members after the second session.

Having a well-balanced group size based on the number of facilitators is important to the overall functioning of the group. You and the group members will benefit by carefully structuring the group size.

Length of Sessions

The sessions in this guidebook are designed for a two-and-a-half-hour period of time. For the most part, the material in the *Format* section of each session can be completed in the first sixty to seventy-five minutes of group time. The exceptions are the sessions on Patterns of Abuse and Anger about Abuse, which tend to take most of the time period. See each activity for additional information on the amount of time needed to successfully address these two topics.

Some topic sessions have more information or exercises than can be realistically covered in sixty to seventy-five minutes. Only you can determine how much of each session to use. When you determine that the individual session needs to be reduced in size, you can then choose which information is to be included or omitted. By being aware of the length of each topic session, you can allow time for a break and individual time-taking each week.

Open-ended versus Closed-ended Groups

A *closed-ended* group usually has a specific starting and ending date, with a designated number of members assigned to the group. The members begin and end the group together, with no members being added to the group after the second session. An *open-ended* group may have open starting and ending dates. It typically starts with a core group of members but will allow members to be added during the course of the group.

First, let us say that there is no one "right" way of conducting groups for women who have been abused by their male partners. We strongly believe in the group process in terms of effectively helping battered women with their healing process.

Our model is based on a sixteen-week, closed-ended group. It is supplemented by individual counseling sessions and other methods of support and advocacy.

There are some advantages and disadvantages to consider if you are in a position to offer closed- or open-ended groups. Our bias is obvious, since we offer closed-ended groups as our primary counseling mode. Below we list only a few of the things to consider in conducting closed-ended groups.

1. The first advantage to a closed-ended women's group is that all members experience all stages of the group process at the same time. On the first night of group, everyone experiences various anxieties and feelings, and develops their trust for the group all at the same time. Often in the first group meeting the women develop an incredible bond with each other that establishes an immediate trust and cohesiveness for the group. Sometimes in open-ended groups, in which new members are added over time, the trust and cohesiveness of the group may be in constant flux.

2. A second advantage to a closed-ended group is that the group activities can be planned and introduced according to the group's needs or progress. The exercises are new for all the group members and work very well because of the fact that all members are experiencing the exercise for the first time together. In an open-ended group you may find that by having to repeat previous activities for new members some of the impact is lost for members who have already participated in that activity. However, in an open group, the role of the long-term members shifts to being more facilitators of the activity than participants, giving both the new and the old members a different experience. In open-ended groups that are working well, the staff counselor relies more heavily on the long-term members of the group to provide the leadership for the group.

3. In closed-ended groups there are clearer phases of the group, so members can experience the three distinct phases of groups: beginning, middle, and ending phases.

While we prefer closed-ended groups, we are aware that this is not always a viable or practical option for many programs. For example, battered women's shelters that facilitate groups are usually serving women on a short-term basis with very high turnover. Programs that have sporadic attendance or a limited number of women attending at any given time also would not be in a good position to offer closed-ended groups.

Open-ended groups have many strengths and are also an important and necessary way to help serve battered women. Both open- and closed-ended groups require effective group counseling skills and practices. With minor changes, most of the sessions in this book can be adapted for use in open-ended groups, as can the accompanying journal.

Group Setting

A safe setting is an important factor that increases the success of the group. Safety of the women is critical. Women who do not feel that the setting in which they meet is safe may be severely distracted, inhibiting their ability to focus in the group session.

The group room itself should be inviting and preferably away from the child care room (if applicable) in a quiet place in the facility. The room should be private and safe from distractions. Chairs should be reasonably comfortable. You will need a chalkboard or a writing easel and other materials for your drawing and writing activities.

Support versus Therapy

The Wilder women's groups are typically facilitated by professional, credentialed staff who have bachelor's or master's degrees. The majority of our staff have been educated and trained in psychology, social work, counseling, women's studies, or similar disciplines. We have also had staff with no degrees but with life experiences and personal strengths that made them a valued resource to our participants. Since the start of the program, we have also used student interns from the local colleges, community volunteers, and other professionals.

Many ideas exist about the issue of counseling versus therapy for battered women. Some positions on this issue follow.

- One position suggests that when women who have been abused are told they need counseling, therapy, or treatment, the implication is that there is something wrong with them: Saying women need counseling places blame or responsibility on the woman for the man's violence; it suggests that if the woman would change her behavior, she would stop being abused. Certainly this position warrants serious consideration. The last thing that anyone working with women who have been abused would want to perpetuate is the myth that the victim has something to do with her partner's abuse.

- A second position suggests that women who seek counseling for being victims of male battering may be (and have been) labeled with a clinical mental health diagnosis or other stigmatizing labels, which can have potentially serious ramifications. For example, in some instances a woman may not be eligible for life or medical insurance if she has had a certain diagnosis related to being abused. One can easily see how a woman may be re-victimized for a crime that has been committed against her.

  Women who have been battered and have sought counseling have also had to defend themselves in the courts. Perpetrators have used the courts and legal counsel to question the stability or suitability of the woman who has received professional psychiatric or therapeutic assistance. It has also been suggested that the woman has a weakness or deficiency in her character, as evidenced by her seeking counseling.

There have also been cases in which the woman's parenting or coping skills are questioned because she has received counseling. The children are usually caught in the middle in these cases. The courts may often be unaware or unenlightened about the extent of the violence that has occurred.

- Another issue has been a "grass-roots" versus a "professional" approach toward serving battered women. The discussion revolves around who is more qualified or knowledgeable to work with victims of abuse.

- Yet another debate is what services should receive emphasis: shelter and advocacy or counseling and therapy.

  Unfortunately, many of these discussion have pitted women against women, "grass-roots" women advocates against women who are "professional" counselors and therapists. The outcome of these discussions is unknown. Hopefully the listening and learning will continue, and battered women will reap the rewards of this difficult work.

Women who have been abused have greatly benefited from the therapeutic model described in this manual. It blends therapy, education, support, and advocacy into a structured and purposeful intervention that aids in the empowerment of women and affirms them in their healing process.

Facilitator Teams

There is no one way to facilitate groups. It is important to consider the different possibilities when deciding what outcomes you would like to achieve. We have trained numerous interns and staff facilitators over the past fifteen years. We have learned a great deal from the different skills and styles that all of the facilitators, new and experienced, had to offer.

We recommend a team of two facilitators. We have facilitated women's domestic abuse groups with different combinations including one female facilitator, two female facilitators, and one female and one male facilitator. We categorically discourage having *only* a male facilitator.

In all cofacilitated groups the participants benefit from the perspectives of two counselors versus one. Sometimes one counselor may not be able to reach some members of the group, while the other facilitator can. In cofacilitated groups, the facilitators devote much time to processing the group sessions. Usually, it takes more time and work for two people to lead groups, compared to solo facilitation, but the results typically are much better overall when there are two facilitators. The support factor alone for each of the facilitators makes the additional investment of time and energy worthwhile. For these and other reasons, we prefer cofacilitated groups whenever possible.

Two Female Facilitators
The most common choice is having two female counselors facilitate the group. Group members are comfortable with this combination and benefit from the modeling of two women.

Two women facilitators can provide an excellent opportunity to provide diversity to the group. This would include such variables as: age, culture or ethnic group, personal life experiences, and other valuable attributes. Individual styles and unique skills of the two women facilitators can create an insightful and empowering group experience with women in leadership roles.

Female and Male Cofacilitators

In our experience, the combination of one female and one male facilitator (given the right pairing) is the most desirable. While programs that work with battered women may primarily employ female workers, there are many benefits to using a male counselor in a women's domestic abuse group.

One of the primary benefits is that the women can hear and observe a male who:

- Displays clear boundaries

- Shows sensitivity and support for women's needs and issues

- Displays appropriate compassion and empathy

- Acknowledges that women are not responsible for their male partner's abusive behavior

The decision to do female/male cofacilitation in women's domestic abuse groups warrants serious attention. The female facilitator must determine the workability of such a combination. If not done thoughtfully and properly, the potential for serious harm exists. On the other hand, if all factors are in place, we have found it to be the most effective method of service; we have only positive outcomes to report. Consider the following when facilitating a women's domestic abuse group with female and male facilitators:

- Careful selection of the male cofacilitator.

- The male facilitator's role in the group is clearly defined. He should have a secondary role, with the female cofacilitator as the lead facilitator of the group. The male facilitator should follow her direction.

- The male facilitator must seek feedback from the female facilitator and also from the women in the group as to how his presence and comments are affecting the group.

- The male facilitator must understand that most women participants have experienced men in positions of power within their relationships. Therefore, the male facilitator must be keenly aware of his presence and impact on the group.

Once this team is established, there are other unique issues that must be addressed. The first one is, "When does the male facilitator begin working with the client?" We conduct individual intake sessions with each client prior to the beginning of a group. When there is a male/female team, we believe that the male counselor should be involved from the beginning, including the individual sessions. If this is not possible or practical, the female counselor could conduct the intake session and inform the client that the group will be cofacilitated by a male staff member. The counselor may ask the client about any feelings or concerns she might have about having a male facilitator in the group.

The counselor should communicate the purpose and some of the advantages of having a male facilitator in the group. She can also share her experiences working with a male cofacilitator. If the client is still uncomfortable, the female counselor could ask the client to give it some more thought and decide what would be best for her. The counselor could offer her a different group (if available) that does not have a male cofacilitator.

A key factor in helping women feel more comfortable with the idea of a male cofacilitator is often how it is presented by the female counselor. It is a normal response for women to feel initial discomfort with a male cofacilitator, but this usually subsides within the first or second group session.

One Female Facilitator

Single facilitation is another method we use in our women's domestic abuse groups. Most of the time this condition results because we do not have other available staff or interns. Single facilitation can be very effective and offers a few advantages over cofacilitation. Single facilitation is more time-efficient and can be more economical. It is also easier for one facilitator to determine the agenda, curriculum, and direction of the group. The facilitator doesn't need to concern herself with a conflict of styles or personalities with a cofacilitator and can focus all her attention on the group. Some facilitators actually prefer facilitating groups alone, trading some of the advantages that coleadership may provide for the advantages of solo facilitation.

Group Members Who Know Each Other

Depending on how large a community you serve, you may find that some of the women in the group know one another.

In a medium-sized city such as the one we serve, this situation occurs somewhat infrequently. But in a smaller community individuals are more likely to know one another. We have even experienced situations where participants who were related to each other found themselves in the same group.

This situation can present a difficult dilemma and awkward moment for individuals, the group, and the group facilitator. It could also result in humiliation and cause a serious loss of privacy and exposure for the women involved. Unfortunately, there is no practical way to prevent this situation and there are only limited solutions for it. Women who seek help from battered women's shelters have experienced a similar dilemma.

If, during introductions at the first group meeting, it's acknowledged that certain members know one another, the group facilitator could ask a few questions. For example:

- How do you know each other?
- Do you see being in the same group as an issue?

If it seems inappropriate to go any further with the questions in the group, the facilitator may need to ask to talk with the women outside of the group for a few minutes. The way the facilitator deals with this situation is being observed and processed by everyone in the group. The sensitivity and respect displayed by the facilitators is very important and shows how participant confidentiality and privacy issues will be addressed in the group.

One or both members may choose to attend a different group, if available, or wait until the next group begins. Develop a plan to prepare the group members and staff for this experience. Each participant's privacy must be held in high regard in order to provide a safe and respectful environment for everyone.

Group Member and Facilitator Who Know Each Other

Occasionally, group and staff members know each other. This also has been rare in our experience. Typically, a staff person may have attended school with a group member or possibly knew her from another setting (work, old neighborhood).

When this relationship is acknowledged, an open discussion will help determine to what extent this previous knowledge of each other will affect the woman and the facilitator. Both parties should carefully consider their thoughts and feelings about this situation. After considering both parties' comments and concerns, the facilitator should decide if the woman can best be served in her particular group. If not, other resources should be located. It is important to work through the decision with the participant to ensure that she understands the reasoning behind it. Being honest with her may lessen the possibility that she will feel victimized again by the process. She is very vulnerable. In this scenario, she has again been exposed. Whether or not the final decision is that she attends the group, she will probably have a number of thoughts and feelings regarding this encounter with a person from her past.

These are not easy decisions to make. The highest level of professional ethics and boundaries should be upheld when working with any participant who seeks services. When facing difficult issues, seek outside help from a supervisor, colleagues, or others who can be trusted to give sound guidance or consultation.

Groups Not Bonding

In our experience, women's groups usually bond quickly and effortlessly. Most of this success can be attributed to the women themselves. They have all been victims of violence from their intimate male partners. This can be an extremely powerful bond and is the moving force behind the group experience.

When groups do not initially bond well, we move quickly to look for a tangible reason, followed by a solution. One scenario may occur if one or two women immediately take a vocal, dominant role in the group. To the other group members, they may appear very opinionated and possibly intimidating. The other group members may begin to think they will not be able to share their thoughts and feelings because these vocal members tend to monopolize much of the group's time. They might also anticipate that the group facilitator will not be able to manage these group members. The group may feel unsafe or out of control. Facilitators should recognize and quickly strategize ways to address this issue if it occurs.

A second scenario may occur when group members start giving advice to the other members, such as "You should get rid of the jerk, he's never gonna change and you're a fool to stay with him . . . I've been there and I can tell you, you need . . ." Unfortunately, no one can ever know what might be said in the group that could potentially damage the group process or be hurtful to a group member.

In these situations and others, prevention and careful intervention strategies will be keys to establishing or re-establishing group responsibilities and the goals of the group. Referring to the group expectations can be helpful as a starting place.

Attrition

Many reasons exist for attrition in women's domestic abuse groups. Some women are in crisis and have too much happening in their lives to continue with the group. Other women may need to move away from the area for safety reasons. Sometimes medical conditions prohibit a woman from staying in group (pregnancy or childbirth, depression, anxiety, and so on).

Transportation and child-care problems are two common reasons for women dropping out of group. If resources permit, these two issues could be addressed by providing on-site child care or by offering money that would cover child care and transportation costs. It is also possible that other women in the group may offer transportation to group members once the group starts and they are informed of a woman's need.

Other possible reasons for attrition may include the following:

- Hiding group participation from a partner
- Discomfort with the group process
- Conflict with other group members
- Serious mental health issues
- Being overwhelmed by other life situations
- Partner stopping a woman from attending

It is difficult at times not to become discouraged by attrition or attendance problems that may occur in a group. Be sensitive to the barriers and needs of the participants. Creative thinking and problem solving by the facilitators and group members have produced some amazing results.

Group Is Not for Everyone

Group is *not* for everyone. There are many reasons why this method of counseling and support may not meet the needs or be an appropriate choice for some women. Safety, timing, emotional and physical health, and other factors must be taken into consideration. It is critical to consider these and other issues in determining the appropriateness of group counseling for each and every participant.

Power of the Group Experience

On the other hand, our experience also has shown us the power of the group. For many women, the thought of sharing their abusive situations with strangers can initially be very intimidating. However, shortly into the group, even as early as the first group session, women often express how significant the group experience has become for them. They realize for the first time, when they see a group of intelligent, articulate, nurturing women who have experienced similar abuse, that *they are not alone.* They also feel empowered by the process to make their *own* critical decisions and feel supported in those decisions—*whatever they are.*

We have seen dramatic changes in many women during the relatively short sixteen-week group process. Time and time again, women will describe their group as being one of the most powerful and helpful experiences of their lives.

Using Inclusive Language

At first glance, the concept of using inclusive language may seem unimportant. But using inclusive language means that as women, we are all in this journey together. (When there is a male cofacilitator, the inclusive language is modified as appropriate.) None of us has escaped being abused in one way or another. At a minimum, we have all been abused as females by the media, billboards, religion, magazines, the judicial system, the educational system, and more. To understand and develop problem-solving strategies related to abuse means we have specific and inclusive language to use and *not* to use.

Using the words "we," "us," and "our" when talking about women as a group is crucial. For example, suppose you want to make a point about what it is like for women to be raped. We'll assume this has not been a part of your experience. If you refer to "you women" who have been raped or "the women" who have been raped, or "those women" who have been raped, you have just set yourself apart as different, privileged, special, and a nonmember of this group.

The lesson here is *never* to talk about "you women," "the women," and "these/those women." The pronouns and descriptors are not inclusive and can be offensive and demeaning to group members, making them feel ashamed about their abuse. It is very acceptable to talk in terms of "we as women" when addressing any issues related to concerns of females.

Women, as a whole group, are in this fight for change together. Some may not yet recognize this. Some women see abuse and its consequences as something that happens only to other women. They separate themselves from the reality of abuse and want to define it as "you who are" and "we who are not" abused. As facilitators of women's groups, we must learn the difference between inclusive and non-inclusive language and understand the meaning and difference in our hearts.

Special Needs

Women who are visually, physically, or hearing impaired and are being battered are in an extremely difficult position. In addition to all the obstacles and barriers that battered women encounter in their efforts to be free of the violence, women with special needs face several more.

We try to connect women with the appropriate resources to best meet their needs. Shelters, intervention projects, or information and referral hot lines have a wealth of information about specialized services for women with special needs. We also have a resource book that lists different agencies that provide specialized services for participants. Local crisis hot lines can provide information about services and agencies in your area. Or there may be a resource book available listing the various agencies and programs that provide services in your area.

Although we have only provided services to a limited number of women who have hearing or sight impairments, it has proven to be a valuable service. An American Sign Language (ASL) interpreter has been made available for hearing-impaired women in the groups. Our experience has been extremely positive in that the interpreters have been very willing to work with our counselor(s) and the group members to provide a comfortable and accessible place for the hearing-impaired woman to receive the full benefit of our women's program, including the group experience.

Before a hearing-impaired woman enters the group, the counselor should spend time with the interpreter to describe the women's program and to plan how to best serve her. During the first session, allow time for introducing the interpreter and discussing as a group how the hearing-impaired member would have the most positive and helpful group experience. This might include techniques such as slowing down the discussion process periodically. Also, allow time for the hearing-impaired woman to present her issues through her interpreter as these issues arise.

Women with special needs face other important issues that are compounded by abuse. Certainly the sense of physical and emotional isolation is strong for women who are being battered and are already somewhat isolated from a hearing- or sight-oriented world.

We are not the experts at providing services to women with special needs. What we have attempted to do is provide the best possible access and information to women with special needs without interfering in their choices about meeting their own needs.

One situation in which we have found it difficult to provide effective service is when English is a woman's second language. We have attempted to use an interpreter in the women's groups, but found it too distracting. It may be possible in some settings, though, to conduct a bilingual group. Unfortunately, there may not be services available in your geographic area for women who do not speak or understand English. Again, our staff provides a current list of resources that may better serve the woman's special needs.

Substance Abuse

Alcohol and other chemical abuse cannot be ignored as it pertains to domestic abuse. Some battered women indicate that chemical use or abuse has played a significant part in their partner's abusive behaviors. Our position is that chemical abuse is one issue that must be addressed and that battering behavior is a separate issue. There are many men who batter who do not abuse chemicals or may even be recovering from chemical abuse but still are abusing their partners (verbally, emotionally, physically, or sexually). We also know from women's reports that their partner's abuse has the potential to increase or become more severe with his chemical use.

Our women's program has worked with some women who have had active chemical abuse issues. If a woman states in the initial intake that she uses chemicals to cope with her abusive situation, she is asked to make a commitment that she will not use them on the day of group.

If chemical issues do surface for the women, we explore referral options to appropriate services that deal specifically with chemical issues. If the woman does not want to address her chemical abuse problem, we determine whether she can continue to be served in the domestic abuse program. Each case is considered on an individual basis.

Ideally, we prefer that women address chemical issues first and then enter the women's domestic abuse group. The counselor has the discretion, however, to determine what would work best for the individual. This is not an easy situation to deal with given the complexity of the need for help and support regarding victimization. At the same time, a woman's active chemical issues may interfere with her ability to receive help and support regarding her victimization by her partner.

Consider this issue carefully. Our experience tells us that there is no one clear-cut answer. In a perfect world, addressing the chemical abuse first would be ideal. However, there are very few perfect scenarios when it comes to dealing with chemical abuse or battering.

Societal Myths and Messages

There are countless lists, articles, and books that address the societal myths and messages that exist in male/female intimate relationships. Many of these can be applied to the issues that face women in abusive relationships. Whether the myths and messages are perpetuated by society, men, women, or institutions, they continue to affect how we relate to one another.

For a woman who has been abused, these myths and messages can continue to victimize her and keep her trapped in an abusive relationship. The common beliefs or myths that continue to surface about women who are abused include such things as: they are crazy; they are masochistic; they provoke the man's violence; it's only a "certain" few who are being abused; they are ignorant or deserving of the abuse; and if what's happening is that bad, they should just leave. These and other beliefs regarding victims of abuse are voiced by many in our society, including some professionals who are in a position to help victims—counselors, clergy, policymakers, judges, and doctors. We have been asked questions and heard statements from people in all walks of life that reflect the attitudes listed above. There are many experiences and facts that do not support any of these myths. However, it continues to be a daily challenge to stop the perpetuation of these beliefs, especially when there are so many forces working to promote them.

The pressure of our history, institutions, media, entertainment, and lifestyles on women, men, children, and teens is incredibly strong. The messages that men must be aggressive, rich, dominant, breadwinners, macho, and in charge not only continue to promote unhealthy or abusive attitudes towards women, but also set men up for unhealthy, unhappy, and potentially abusive lives. To think that these messages for boys or men went out of date in the 1950s is simply not true. The modern, "more sensitive" man of the 21st century looks remarkably like the macho heroes of days gone by. One only needs to spend an evening watching TV, looking at the top box office movies or video rentals, or ads in a popular magazine to discover the same stereotypes, only in a more modern and provocative form.

This bombardment of the new and improved look at male/female relationships is not only aimed at boys and men. The messages that young girls and women continue to see on screen and in print once again are familiar in looks, if not in style. The focus is still on women's body image, sex, submissiveness, and spending time and money on attracting and satisfying the opposite sex. Yes, there are many messages that have gotten women "out of the kitchen" with greater independence—however, not without consequences. Some of these have been used against women by their abuser. For example, "This house is a pigpen; it's that job you got that's messing up our lives." The alleged breakdown of the American family has more than once been wrongly blamed on the changing role of women in our culture.

The overt and subtle myths and messages ultimately will determine the amount of violence that our society will face in the future. Violence against women is gaining more attention, primarily through the increase in reporting and awareness. Much of this awareness can be attributed to the work of battered women, battered women's shelters, battered women's advocate groups, coalitions, and others. Unfortunately, the work is not finished and, in fact, continues to become increasingly difficult. We must continue to challenge the myths and messages that support the beliefs and images that are harmful to all human beings. There are no winners when it comes to promoting violence of any kind toward anyone.

Women Who Have Perpetrated Abuse

Helping women who have perpetrated abuse is an extremely sensitive and controversial issue as it relates to women who have been battered. Attitudes vary widely, from "women never are perpetrators of abuse" to "women are as abusive as men." In our experience, neither of these views is accurate.

The primary focus of our women's groups is to address the victimization issues of the women we serve. Almost without fail, when we conduct training for professionals or communities, we are asked, "What about women who are abusive?" Male perpetrators in the men's group also ask this question.

We believe that anyone has the capacity to be abusive toward someone else. Men, women, adolescents, and children certainly can be and have been abusive. However, our experience and formal statistical data regarding domestic homicides, emergency-room admissions, child protection cases, and criminal court records indicate that the overwhelming majority of domestic abuse is perpetrated by males. In the case of intimate relationships, the victims are significantly more often women and children, not men.

There are, however, women who have been abusive towards their intimate male or female partners, their children, or both. Our response is that abuse is never justified, no matter who perpetrates it. We hold anyone accountable for their own behavior. We have worked with many women who have been perpetrators, some of whom have committed serious crimes of assault, malicious punishment of a child, and even murder. We have found that, *without exception,* women who have committed abuse or violent acts against others have also been victimized themselves. In most cases, the abuse has been extensive and long-term. This is not to say we excuse the abusive behavior. What we offer in these situations is support, information, and counseling that focuses on nonviolent alternatives.

Most abusive women enter our women's groups openly admitting to their own abuse in all of its forms. They also are afraid of becoming more abusive (especially towards their children) and ask for help on this issue. So often there is a public misconception that women who are battered go into groups with other battered women and bash and blame men. In our experience, such women are often overly focused on themselves, question their own behavior, and feel extremely ashamed about what they have identified as their abuse toward their children or partner.

Self-defense is another question that comes up in group and in public opinion. We have frequently heard women describe a situation in which they hit or pushed their partners. They often feel terrible about it and identify it as abusive and wrong. However, most observers would form a different picture—one of self-defense to escape or prevent more serious injury. A woman often will fail to mention her partner's behaviors that occurred prior to her behavior. In this case, others may view the woman as having an equal or mutual part in the violence.

We suggest that often what might look like mutual abuse is not. We must first understand that *not* everything is equal here, given all that is known about male violence against women. The facts are that most women don't stand a chance in abusive situations. Male perpetrators of violence, once they recognize their denial, will often readily state that their partners are no match for them physically.

In some instances, women will describe their actions as a last resort. "I just couldn't take it anymore," "I lost it!" "I just started screaming or pounding on his chest or hit him with a pan or . . . " They express a sense of total frustration, anger, revenge, or hate. Women may talk about their behavior in terms of "getting him before he gets me." They feel there is nothing left to lose—it's the last straw.

The heated discussion of women's so-called mutual violence towards their male partner distracts from the real issue. Bluntly put, women are being bruised, beaten, and killed in staggering numbers. The perpetrators of this abuse are most often men, more specifically, the intimate male partner. **No one deserves to be abused. Anyone can be abusive.** How we work, judge, assume, condone, believe, express, and determine what is to be done can take us down many paths. The question of who gets to decide what is the right or wrong path will continue to challenge all of our minds and spirits.

Putting One's Hope in Treatment of the Abusive Partner

Women often want their partners to get treatment for their abuse. For women who are still in their relationships or hope to remain involved, treatment for their partner can be a primary concern.

Some women think that treatment holds the magic cure for their abusive partner. "If only he would go to treatment, things would be fine." It is easy to understand why women would hold this hope for their partners. Abusers are not abusive twenty-four hours a day. There are many qualities that women describe about their partners that contribute to the hope that the relationship will work—if only the abuse would stop.

Facilitators addressing this issue face many potential pitfalls when they try to give honest and unbiased information. For virtually all treatment beginnings, there is the hope for overcoming the adversity or problem, no matter how big it is. Facilitators need to be prepared to address this question or the hope that men who batter can and will change.

Not enough is known about men's domestic abuse treatment outcomes. The general consensus among people working in this area is that battering will not just "go away" on its own. In fact, unless there is some kind of intervention (arrest, jail, counseling), the abuse often increases in severity over time. Most of this information has come from battered women and from men who have described their experiences as perpetrators of domestic abuse.

We attempt to give a balanced and honest response to questions about men ending their violence as a result of treatment. This includes making women aware that treatment may or may not work for their partner. In our experience in providing counseling to thousands of men who batter, changing their abusive behavior in all of its forms is a long-term and difficult process, one that many do not complete. It requires a major commitment to change. No program can offer a magic or guaranteed cure.

For women whose partners are or have been in treatment, we always encourage using their own judgment or instincts about their partner's progress. We emphasize that their insights and feelings have directed and guided their ability to survive in the relationship. These gut-level beliefs and intuitions can and must be trusted. This information can be combined with the new awareness they have gained from group about the abuse they have experienced.

Safety and Protection

Safety for women in abusive relationships will be an overriding theme for all the group sessions. Group facilitators must remain aware of, and talk about, how women can stay safe while they make decisions about what to say, what to do, and how to act when interacting with their abusive partners.

We do not offer a separate group session on safety and protection. This is due to the individualized need and timing that is so important in discussing or implementing safety plans. Our experience at Wilder has indicated that this topic is not always applicable for many group participants and thus can be addressed as needed during the individual time taking portion of the session or when a woman is in a crisis related to her safety.

A protection and safety plan for an individual woman who feels she is in danger should be personalized according to her needs and circumstances. The situations that most often require safety planning include: living with an abusive partner, planning to leave an abusive partner, or dealing with stalking behaviors.

Possibly the single most important item that the facilitator can communicate about safety is *advance preparation*. Advance preparation means helping women to think about situations they may encounter so they can prepare themselves to respond safely. It is important to talk to women about what kinds of resources need to be in place to best address their individual safety needs. Suggest that they think about what has worked in the past, who their support system might be, what cues or signs might indicate that abuse is escalating, and who in their community they could turn to for help.

The ideas and approaches to be considered for effective safety plans are too numerous to be detailed here, but the following list outlines some basic suggestions:

- Plans for looking out for children's best interests
- Telephone availability (cellular or portable, if possible)
- Hidden cash for emergency purposes
- Extra keys for the car and house
- Copies of important papers/information
- Phone numbers of emergency contacts
- Clothing items packed for quick departures
- Codes with friends/neighbors to call for help
- Plans for a place to go when leaving

When you are helping a woman formulate a protection and safety plan, it is crucial to communicate that you are concerned for her safety but that you do not expect her to follow any certain plan. The goal of the safety plan is *only* that she be prepared in advance as much as possible to carry out any safety decision she may decide to make.

Discussing safety plans can occur either in one-on-one counseling or in the group setting. If done in group, other members who have left their abusive partners will often share what worked and what didn't. Again, it will be important for the counselor to remind the group that what may work or feel comfortable for one person may not apply for another.

For further information on safety and protection planning, we recommend *Getting Free: You Can End Abuse and Take Back Your Life* by Ginny NiCarthy, available from Seal Press, 3131 Western Avenue, Suite 410, Seattle, WA 98121, 1-800-754-0271.

Group Phone Lists

Should the facilitator encourage or discourage groups from sharing their phone numbers on a list? This is a tough call and a controversial matter for many group facilitators. There are positive and negative aspects to either decision.

The positive side of group members sharing a phone list is that individual members can get needed support between group sessions. This can be a good thing for members who understand good boundaries and are respectful of the availability of the person they have contacted for support.

The negative aspects of phone lists are more numerous. Many events can occur that have the potential of throwing the group off balance. One is group members forming friendships outside of group which don't go well after a short time. If bad feelings develop between two people, one of the members may feel a need to drop out of the group. The group balance can be disrupted when a member suddenly drops out with no closure.

Another is when boundaries between members outside of the group are not well defined, members may ask the facilitator to do something about the group member with poor boundaries, for example, calling another group member every day. This can become problematic for the facilitator as issues develop with little time to address them during the group. In addition, the facilitator needs to have the group in balance without sounding punitive to the members.

A creative way to address the issue of a group phone list is to discourage it for the first half of the group. Explain the problems that can occur with a phone list and suggest that the group wait until eight or so sessions have taken place before sharing their phone numbers. You can offer a couple of examples of how things have gone poorly in the past for some groups. You can also ask for some of their ideas or concerns on this issue. Most members will understand the potential boundary problems.

As the group facilitator, you can take an even stronger position and tell members that it is a group expectation that they not contact each other outside of group. Again, you will need to explain the downside of members being in contact so they understand how this may disrupt the group process.

If a phone list is generated, it is important for the members to protect the information from being lost or stolen. It may present a serious problem if the phone numbers and names of the women fall into the wrong hands. The members need to know that the information is confidential, and every effort should be made to keep it safe.

Finally, you can let the group decide if it's a good idea to generate a phone list after you explain the potential problems that can arise. Most women can handle a phone list appropriately and have good boundaries when it comes to contacting other group members. You can encourage women to talk with the group facilitator if any such problems do occur. This is not "tattling." Rather, it is assertive behavior and effective problem solving that can prevent group members from developing negative feelings and dropping out of group.

Use of Videos and Films

There are several videos on the market that could be shown in the women's groups. We generally use videos or films sparingly during the sixteen-week group. The main reason is that there is not enough time as it is to do all of the group sessions that we have determined to be important in the women's group process.

If you prefer to show a video or film, preview it and decide on the purpose of showing it in group. Give group members permission to take care of themselves while viewing the film. This could mean that they would leave the room or "zone out" if the material in the film becomes too intense. Choose some discussion questions to present to the group and allow enough time for discussion after the video is shown. Depending on the content of the video, the impact could be quite powerful for some of the women in the group. In fact, "flashbacks" or a resurfacing of trauma may occur. Whenever a video or film is shown, we recommend that the women's counselor stay in the room with the group. You may need to stop the video if you sense a reaction that could be putting group members in a state of emotional distress. If you decide to use videos at all, consider showing them towards the later stages of the group (tenth or twelfth week) rather than earlier in the group.

Security in the Building

We have a security staff person at the front entrance of the building who monitors those who enter the facility. No one is allowed in the building during the group time except the women and their children. (See Child Care section on page 28). We conduct men's and women's groups on different nights of the week. The security staff monitors the parking lot and surrounding area to ensure these areas are safe. Upon completion of each group session, the security person escorts all women and children to their vehicles to ensure their safe departure.

Not all programs may be able to provide this kind of service. There may be other ways to ensure the safety of the women while they're attending their group. Volunteers from area churches or communities may be available to provide this service.

It is important to clarify to the security staff (particularly male security staff) their role, professional boundaries with clients, and the significance of their job. Alert the security person of any potential threatening or dangerous situations regarding an abusive partner showing up at the building site. Give the security staff personal and auto identification of the abusive partner to help prevent a serious incident.

If you use nonprofessional security staff such as volunteers, they should also receive specific training and instructions on how to perform their duties. We cannot emphasize too strongly the importance of proper training for individuals providing security services for battered women and their children.

Mutual Arrest

The increase in numbers of mutual arrests in domestic assault cases is a growing concern. This is an important issue as it applies to providing counseling services for women who have been arrested for mutually assaulting their male partners.

Women who have been arrested for mutual assault need a supportive advocate to discuss their feelings about the arrest experience. Often a woman who has been arrested for a domestic assault feels ashamed, embarrassed, confused, or angry. She may feel betrayed by the system that she expected would protect her from the violence of her partner but which instead has found her guilty of "mutual" abuse. It is a complex and confusing message to a woman who has clearly been victimized yet is now having to answer for her alleged violence towards her abuser.

We have found that the majority of women acknowledge their own behavior in the incident and have no interest in hiding their actions toward their partner. What does surface is the woman's fear that the system she had hoped would protect her and her children is no longer reliable. She believes the system now views her as part of the problem and no longer a credible person. Knowing that the law cannot or may not protect her from future abuse places her in a more vulnerable position. She may feel terrified and isolated. These feelings need to be explored in a safe, nurturing environment such as the group setting or an individual session. She may need additional resources and support as well.

Finally, women who need help to deal with their own abusive behaviors require help that is sensitive to the needs of women who are both being abused and also being abusive in their own behaviors. This type of resource may be difficult to find. We have developed a specialized program to serve women who are both victims and perpetrators of abuse.

Even when women are arrested for assault on their partners because "physical evidence" (scratch marks, cuts, bruises) is substantiated, we hesitate to assume the woman is a perpetrator. For many women who have received systematic abuse by their partners, self-defense or an outburst of retaliation does not necessarily define them as a perpetrator of abuse. We do not support abusive behavior by anyone. Still, we must understand the context in which a woman may act.

Group Evaluations

Evaluations of the group by the participants are an integral part of the group experience. Final group evaluations are essential, and weekly or midpoint evaluations or both can be very helpful. Each member should have the opportunity to express her thoughts and feelings about the group anonymously. The evaluations enable you and your program to assess the effectiveness of the group and to make changes and improvements as needed.

Weekly evaluations can be either oral or written. They should not take more than two or three minutes of group time. The decision to do or not do weekly evaluations will depend on the style of the group leader. Midpoint evaluations are a good idea, as there is still time in the group to make changes that might improve the group. Midpoint evaluations should be completed around the eighth session of a sixteen-week group and should not take more than five to ten minutes to finish.

Final group evaluations are the most comprehensive of the evaluations and should take approximately ten to fifteen minutes to complete. They should be designed to convey as much as possible about how the members viewed the group in terms of effectiveness, helpfulness, general satisfaction, and so on. All written evaluations should be anonymous and voluntary but strongly encouraged, so that you as the group leader and your program, can benefit from how the group members experienced the group. Stress that you are seeking their candid responses.

Sample evaluation forms are provided on pages 181–184.

Group Sessions

Cluster

Essential Beginnings

Introduction to Group

Goals

In this session, participants will:

1. Create a supportive and safe atmosphere in the group.
2. Understand the purpose and philosophical principles of the Women's Domestic Abuse Program.
3. Begin to make connections with group peers.
4. Establish group expectations.
5. Begin the process of addressing personal issues and concerns.
6. Become comfortable in the group setting.
7. Anticipate attending the second group session.

Format

This session helps both the facilitators and the group members introduce themselves and begin the process of getting comfortable in the group. The first session also covers group ground rules that will govern expectations and operating rules for the remainder of the meetings.

1. Name Game

Begin the group by greeting the members and telling them that since there is a great deal to be accomplished at this first session, you want to get started even though one or two members may be a little late. Suggest that before anything else is done, it is important to get to know each other's names.

Say your name and ask the first person to your right to say her name and your name. The next person will say her name, the name of the person next to her, and your name. Continue with this process, going around the circle until the last participant must name everyone in the circle. This game is a good icebreaker and starts the supportive process. At the end, you can ask if anyone else would like to repeat everyone's name again. Usually someone will volunteer.

2. Group Exercise

Tell the group you would like to go around the circle and have each person say one word on how she felt about coming to group today. It works well if you, as the leader, begin the process by saying: "I feel . . ." Then ask the person to your right or left to say how she feels. Expect a range of feelings, from curious to anxious to scared. (Note: Tell the group that at this first session you, as the facilitator, will begin the exercises. In the future, you will not be doing that.)

3. Facilitator Introductions

Introduce yourself briefly by, for example, telling how long you've worked in this field, what your group experience is, and how you feel about working with women. If you are new at facilitating groups or working with domestic abuse, don't hesitate to share this. Women's groups are very supportive of group leaders.

Next, if there is a cofacilitator, ask her to introduce herself. If the cofacilitator is an intern or volunteer, be sure that fact is included.

4. "The Big Wind Blows" Game

Announce to the group that this game is being played to get to know each other a little and to get comfortable by standing up and moving around. As in musical chairs, there should be one less chair in the circle than there are people. (Remove your chair and ask members to round out the circle.)

As the group facilitator, go into the middle of the circle and explain the game as follows: The person in the middle of the circle will make a statement starting with the words "*the big wind blows.*" For example, "*The big wind blows* for anyone who likes pizza." If you like pizza, you must move from your chair and find a new chair. You cannot return to your same chair. The person in the middle looks for an empty chair when people are moving, and a new person ends up in the middle.

Next, tell the group you will now have a practice time and they are to move if what *the big wind blows* about is true for them. Another example might be, *the big wind blows* for anyone who has an older sibling or for anyone who likes to read, who wanted to stay home tonight, or is angry at someone and is afraid to tell them.

Also, the person in the middle can say *hurricane,* at which time all group members must move and find a new chair.

This game can be repeated until each participant has ended up in the middle making some *big wind blows* statement at least one time. Group members generally like this game once it gets started. Facilitators find that it is good for reducing tension in the group.

5. Announcements

Tell the group you have a few announcements to make before you move on to the next exercise. Some things that often need to be included are:

- Name of group—Women's Domestic Abuse Group.
- Length of each session and the number of weeks the group will be held.
- Starting date, ending date, and any dates that will be skipped due to holidays, facilitator vacation, or other reasons.
- Length of breaks and location that group members can use for breaks.
- Smoking policy.
- Bathroom location; coffee, soft drink availability.
- Security in building, if applicable.
- Attendance requirements and any policies regarding absences.
- Importance of beginning group on time. Request that members who know they will be late or absent call and leave a message.
- Importance of attendance at the first four or five sessions. Basic information will be covered that forms the foundation for the entire group.
- Partners of group members are not to be in the building where group is held.
- If child care is provided, give necessary information.
- Group members should feel free to contact facilitators to answer questions or concerns.
- Payment of fees (if applicable).
- Other information as it applies to your program.

6. Toilet Paper Game

To begin this exercise, pass a roll of toilet paper around the group. Ask each group member to take somewhere between five and fifteen sheets. Do not tell them what it is for until this has been completed. Next, tell members that for each sheet they took, they are to share something about themselves with the group. This usually brings moans and groans, so tell them that as the group leader, you will go first. Begin by sharing one item for each sheet you have taken. This is an opportunity to model what kinds of things they might want to share. Examples might be: favorite foods, number of children, leisure activities, likes or dislikes, a bad habit, favorite book, pet ownership, and so on. Then go around the circle until each person has shared something about herself for each sheet of toilet paper she has taken. Help members who get stuck and can't think of anything. By now the group members should begin to feel somewhat relaxed.

7. Eight Program Principles

Begin this part of the session by passing out the journals and asking each participant to turn to the Eight Program Principles on page 2 of the journal.

Read each principle and briefly discuss the philosophy of the program principles as you read them. Ask the group in general what they think of each principle, how they think the principles can work for them, and any examples they would like to share.

1. *Abuse is a learned behavior that has negative consequences for women and children.*
   Our philosophy is that abuse is not contained in one's genetic makeup, but is a behavior that is learned because it frequently works and has rewards. It often works by allowing a person to get what they want by gaining power and control over another.

   The negative consequences for women are numerous and can include the danger of physical harm; health issues such as headaches, nervousness, and ulcers; depression; social isolation; lack of emotional safety; damage to self-esteem; ongoing fear for oneself and one's children.

2. *Abuse is reinforced by our society.*
   From a woman's point of view, abuse may be reinforced by our society through the media, movies, television, music, pornography, sports, advertisements, and commercials, as well as through attitudes of significant people in her life.

3. *Abuse can be passed on from generation to generation.*
   Women relate to this principle because they often have witnessed abuse as children. Women often state that the abuse occurring in their adult lives is exactly what they vowed would never happen. They also report that their abusive partners frequently witnessed abuse as children or were victims of abuse themselves.

4. *There is no justification for abuse.*
   Women do not provoke men into behaving abusively. This is a difficult concept for women, because men frequently tell them the exact opposite, accusing them of being responsible for the abuse. At some level, women usually believe this is true, as they have heard so often that their behaviors are what cause men to act and react violently.

   It is helpful to suggest that throughout this group one goal will be to dispel the idea that a woman's partner is justified in perpetrating abuse against her. The bottom line is that *no one deserves to be abused.*

5. *Women are not responsible for a partner's abusive behavior, nor can they control a partner's abusive behavior.*
   We are all responsible for our own behavior, but we are not responsible for another person's behavior. It does not matter if you burned the roast to a crisp—no one has the right to abuse you. You have the right to make mistakes, make errors in judgment, forget what you're doing, or any

number of other things. None of these behaviors constitutes a justification for abuse. As said before, the bottom line is that there is *no excuse for abuse*.

As women, we tend to believe that if we just don't repeat the event that seemingly caused the abuse in the past, the abuse will not recur. This simply is not true. The rules will change. You have learned not to burn the roast, but you put dinner on the table an hour late, creating a new excuse for the abuse. No matter how hard a woman tries, her partner's behavior is outside her control.

6. *Chemical abuse and domestic violence are two separate issues and need to be addressed separately.*
   Many women believe that chemical use is causing the abuse and that the abuse will not occur if their partners stop using chemicals. It is important to explain to group members why this is not true.

   Acknowledge that chemical use and domestic violence often coexist and exacerbate each other. But there are chemical users who are not perpetrators of violence, and there are men who batter who do not use chemicals. Men who abuse their partners who complete drug-treatment programs will not necessarily stop their violent behavior. They must address that behavior with domestic abuse treatment.

7. *Initially, issues of abuse need to be addressed in a setting that is separate and safe from the abusive person.*
   Many women begin to look for help by seeking joint counseling. We believe this can be unsafe for women until they have had an opportunity to learn about the dynamics of abuse in a safe setting for themselves. It is important that the opportunity exists for a woman to focus on her wants, needs, self-esteem, and ego strength before addressing issues of abuse with her partner (if ever).

   From our experience of working with men who batter, we believe they are not ready for joint counseling until they have accepted responsibility for their abusive behavior and have stopped their battering. Men may pressure their female partner either to seek joint counseling or to give up her separate counseling. This situation will be addressed later on.

8. *Each woman has her own answers and timing for addressing her issues related to abuse.*
   Each group member will be at a different place in her process of acknowledging abuse and figuring out how it is affecting her life. Some women are trying to make decisions about their abusive relationship and may make them during the course of group. Others will need more time to integrate what they are learning and to decide how to apply it to their situation. Patience and unconditional positive regard are musts for both group facilitators and group members. We each have our own internal clock and solutions to our own situations and problems. The group is there to help guide us to finding those answers.

8. Program Goals

Ask the group members to turn to page 2 of the journal for the program goals. Ask the group members to go around the circle and read each goal. This list is not intended for in-depth discussion at this time. Ask if there are any questions or comments on these goals.

Note: These program principles and program goals are a suggested list only. You may want to develop your own.

9. Group Expectations

Next, tell the group that before taking a break, they will establish group expectations. Explain that this is their group and they are responsible for setting the expectations. The following are common expectations that women generally include. Write the expectations on the chalkboard and discuss them as you go along. Some groups will refer to them as the group rules.

Confidentiality
What is said in group must stay in group. This does not mean you cannot talk about what you are learning, but details about other group members cannot be discussed outside of group. Discuss what confidentiality means for the counselors in this setting. Explain the *exceptions* to confidentiality in terms of child abuse, danger of harming oneself or someone else, supervision, requirements of court officials, and so on.

Right to "pass"
Group members can say "pass" at any time when there is a request for participation. This right will be honored.

Begin and end on time
It is the group facilitator's responsibility to see that this happens, but it is helpful to communicate the importance of this to the group members as well.

Punctuality
This is the responsibility of group members. Request that group members call and leave a message if they know they're going to be late.

Respect for others
Respect is given to group members by listening to them, being attentive to what they are saying, and responding in a nonjudgmental and caring manner.

No eating in group
Coffee and soft drinks in group are fine, but eating food or opening packaged food can be very distracting and disruptive.

No drug or alcohol use on the day of group
This is a program policy, and members who do not follow this policy will be asked to leave the group. Note: This has rarely been an issue in our women's domestic abuse groups.

All members share group time

Group members are concerned that no one or two participants monopolize the time available for doing individual group work. This is a valid concern and must be carefully handled by the group facilitator. Group members can help with this as well; ask them how they would like to see this handled if a problem develops.

No advice giving

This is sometimes a difficult expectation to follow, as group members tend to have the answers that they think will help their peers. Stress the importance of giving support and encouragement (not advice) to help people find answers and solutions as a result of the insights they gain in the group.

Break

10. Individual Time Taking

Ask group members to go around the circle and briefly tell of any past group experience. Acknowledge that some group members will know what individual time taking is, but for others it will be a new experience.

Describe time taking to the group (see pages 12–13). Ask if two or three people (or more if time allows) would like time to address a personal concern or issue now. It is important to get this process started at the first session because participants are usually anxious to see how the group process works. Allow plenty of time for two or three people to volunteer.

It is important to remember that moments of silence are okay while group members are thinking about volunteering to take individual time.

11. Closing

During this first session, allow fifteen to twenty minutes for closing. Announce to the group that the session will close by having people respond to a few statements that will help everyone get to know each other further. Write on the chalkboard:

- Who you live with
- Who the abusive person is or was in your life
- One thing you would like to get from this group

Go around the circle, allowing each person to respond to these three statements. Group facilitators can participate in this closing.

Next, ask each person to state:

- How she said she felt at the beginning of group
- How she feels now at the close of group
- How she feels about coming back next week

Announce that next week's session will be on defining abuse.

(Note to facilitator: Record group expectations from the chalkboard to be typed and handed out the following week at group. You may want to make notes about any other important information that may be helpful to you or the group in the future. Include group dates, times, and any other relevant information, on this handout.)

Issues

1. *Many group members and group leaders are nervous and apprehensive at this first session.*
   This is to be expected, and it is important to acknowledge such feelings as soon as possible into the session. As a facilitator, you can talk about your real feelings and the responsibility you feel to guide the group so that it is a good experience for all group members.

2. *Announcements, program principles, and group goals should be covered quickly and efficiently.*
   It is not uncommon for group members to look uncomfortable or detached during these introductory activities in the first half of the session. Move through these at a pace that will allow all housekeeping and other activities to be completed by the break at the midway through the session. This is important because the second half of the session begins the actual support and therapeutic component of the group. Group members are almost always ready for this and anxious to get started on the issues that have brought them together as a group.

3. *It is important to have about forty-five to sixty minutes for individual time taking at this first session.*
   Explain individual time taking briefly and allow ample time for two or three women to use the group for personal time taking. It helps the bonding process begin and helps women become more comfortable in the group as they start to discover that they are not alone with their issues of abuse.

4. *Use appropriate humor and respond positively to the humor of group members.*
   It is important to laugh at this first session. The "getting to know you" exercises can help with this positive release of tension and help women find a comfort level in the group. Caring humor and kind laughter are essential to the well-being of everyone in the group.

5. *Stress the importance of avoiding absences, particularly for the first five sessions.*
   Explain that the first few sessions are committed to learning the basic information and dynamics of abuse. The group will build on this information base during the remaining sessions. Most group members respond to this and will do their best to avoid absences. Mention that some women have been able to attend all sixteen sessions with no absences.

Notes, comments, and observations:

Defining Abuse

Goals

In this session, participants will:

1. Personalize the definition of abuse.

2. Identify specific forms of abuse in four categories: physical, verbal, sexual, and emotional.

3. Begin the process of sharing personal experiences as they identify various kinds of abuse.

4. Begin to recognize that they are not "crazy" or alone with their personal experiences of abuse.

5. State their feelings about having defined abuse in a personal way.

6. Begin to accept that abuse has been a part of their experience and that confusion is a part of abuse.

Format

Defining Abuse is the first of five important sessions in learning about the basics of domestic abuse. It is a time to begin naming what is or has been occurring in the lives of the group members. It will probably give each person in the group a new or different perspective on abuse. Communicate that in this session the topic will be to define abuse according to the experience of this particular group. This will be done by looking at the different kinds of abuse in the four categories of physical, verbal, sexual, and emotional abuse. Explain that there are no "right" answers.

1. Introductions of New Group Members

If there are any new members who are beginning the group at the second session, briefly welcome and introduce them to the group and make them feel as comfortable as possible in this new setting.

Explain that there is not enough time to repeat the more lengthy introductions of the first session. Ask that, during the break, members who attended the first group session tell the new members what they did in group last week.

2. Name Game

Repeat this game for the first few sessions to be sure members learn each other's names.

3. Check-In

In this second session of group, introduce and explain to the participants how the check-in process works (see page 11). Be sure to emphasize that check-in should be held to a minute or less per person and that this is not a time to ask questions or give comments on what group members say.

Ask for a volunteer to start the check-in and go around the circle. Group facilitators should also check in when it is their turn in the process.

4a. Defining Abuse

On the chalkboard, write the four types of abuse in four quadrants. Then ask the group members to offer examples of each type of abuse, either from their own experience or from their general awareness of abuse.

Note: It is appropriate for the facilitator to have a sheet of definitions and types of abuse to refer to at the chalkboard (see Appendix A). Also, ask the cofacilitator or a group volunteer to write down the definitions the group generates, to be typed and handed out at the next session.

PHYSICAL	VERBAL
SEXUAL	EMOTIONAL

Ask the group to begin with types of abuse that might be considered physical abuse. This is the easiest and most concrete form of abuse to define. Confusion sometimes occurs when a woman is experiencing a form of physical abuse in which she is not actually being touched. Examples of this might be: blocking her from leaving or freely moving about, withholding car keys, raising a hand to scare or intimidate, or spitting. Point out that the types of abuse tend to overlap in the four categories.

When brainstorming about types of abuse, allow for plenty of time and silent pauses for women to think about their responses. Some women need to think about whether or not they are ready to share or reveal their experience. It can be embarrassing for any given individual to disclose a particular type of abuse. It is also important to acknowledge the head nods you are seeing as a woman describes a particular abuse, validating the fact that women are not alone with their experience.

Next, ask the group to state different types of verbal abuse. Sometimes it is difficult to differentiate verbal from emotional abuse. As women list types of abuse, you may want to ask them if they can give an example of the abuse to clarify it to the group. This usually works well to get a discussion started and can help the quieter group members participate more spontaneously.

Sexual abuse is often the most difficult area for women to identify and speak up about. It has the potential for being more embarrassing, and some forms are so subtle that they are not thought of as abuse. Identifying sexual abuse usually leads to a discussion of whether or not a partner's refusing to take no for an answer to a request for sexual intercourse is actually a form of sexual abuse. Opinions often vary on this.

Emotional abuse is another area that is sometimes difficult to define. It is less concrete and probably includes all the other abuses already listed. Groups will often need help in identifying specific incidents of emotional abuse. A couple of phrases that may help them think about how they've been emotionally abused are "mind games" or "head games" they may have experienced with their partners.

After identifying the four types of abuse, ask each group member (going around the circle) to comment on:

- What she thinks of the definitions
- How it makes her feel to name abuse as part of her experience

This can take several minutes and may become emotional for some women. It usually brings up the confusion women feel about being abused and often causes them to talk about how they feel they are abusive themselves.

Other points of discussion that can be included in this session are:

- Is any one type of abuse worse than any other type?
- Does emotional abuse have a longer-lasting effect?
- Is there a power imbalance occurring during the abuse?
- Are power and control at the heart of abuse?
- How do we know when our rights are being violated?
- Do we need to talk to someone when we think we are being violated?

Finally, remind group members that *all* their feelings are appropriate. The sense of feeling confused, crazy, and responsible for the abuse are extremely common among women who are abused. Emphasize that the group members will be working to recognize and reduce these feelings over the course of this group.

4b. House of Abuse

Another example of how "Defining Abuse" can be done is by drawing a large house on the chalkboard (see drawing below) which is divided into nine rooms. The facilitator would write in four of the rooms: physical, emotional, verbal, and sexual abuse, and follow the example of first defining physical abuse as suggested in activity 4a. on page 62. The facilitator would then go on to the next rooms (verbal, emotional, and sexual abuse) and complete them one at a time, with the input from the group members.

After filling in the four rooms, the facilitator can suggest that there are other types of abuse they may have experienced. These types may include: social isolation, intimidation, alcohol and drugs, child abuse, male privilege, and others. The facilitator can list these types of abuse in the other rooms of the house as the group participants identify them. Some of these types may have already been identified in the four primary categories (physical, emotional, verbal, and sexual abuse). You can point out to the group that the walls in the house are very thin, and often several types of abuse occur at the same time or in a sequence or series.

The image of the house can be very powerful, since this is where a majority of the abuse may have occurred. Other thoughts and feelings may surface. The house could bring back memories of the abuse a woman witnessed as a child in her own home. A common thought for many women is that if any place should be safe, it is her home. This may trigger an emotional response in terms of lost hopes and dreams of what she had wanted for herself, her children, her partner, and her relationship.

There are other analogies, metaphors, and ideas that can be presented to the group. For example, the facilitator could draw a basement on the house and

House of Abuse

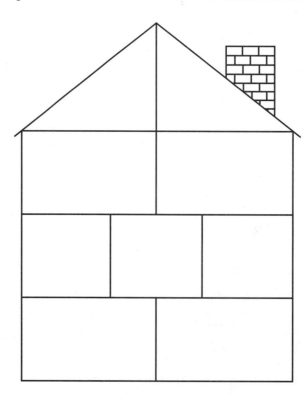

ask the group what they believe might support this kind of house. It may be things like men's attitudes towards women; women's role as defined by a male-dominated society; systems that fail to protect victims; family secrets; or other examples of what is "underneath" the violence.

The facilitator could also ask what supports or keeps the abuse in the house where outsiders may not notice it. Examples may include fear, power, control, and embarrassments. The facilitator could explore with the group the times that the abuse has occurred outside the house and what has happened.

There are a number of questions that the facilitator could ask the group members after the rooms in the house are filled in. One very powerful question is, "How does it feel being on the receiving end of this abuse?" Responses to this question include such things as: afraid, angry, hurt, depressed, vengeful, trapped, imprisoned, helpless, isolated, and many more. The feelings vocabulary list (page 172) may also help women identify their feelings in response to this question.

Another question that could be asked is, "If the perpetrator 'cleaned out' one room in the house, such as stopping his physical abuse, but didn't clean out the other rooms, is he still abusive?"

The facilitator may ask, "How would it feel to be a five-year-old living in this house?" "What would be your concerns?" "What would be the child's concerns?" "How would an adolescent feel?"

There are many other questions and variations of group techniques for this activity that facilitators may want to work on over time. It is important to keep in mind the impact that any of the work regarding defining abuse may have on individuals or the whole group. (See Special Issues section on page 27). In our experience, women who have participated in this activity discover and identify abuse that they had not previously thought of as abuse. This realization of how much abuse they really have endured can have a very powerful effect.

(Note: a reproducible "House of Abuse" can be found on page 185.)

Break

5. Individual Time Taking

6. Closing

Have each participant share with the group one positive thing they can do to take care of themselves after group.

Announce at the close of group that the next week's session will be on Patterns of Abuse. Ask the group to complete the Defining Abuse section in the journal. Remind members that the group process can be very difficult and can trigger unexpected emotions and feelings, so they should be gentle with themselves and care for themselves during the week.

Distribute typed group rules from the introductory session.

Issues

1. *This is a powerful exercise.*
   Women will begin to recognize events in their life as having been abusive, a term they may not necessarily have applied in the past. Defining abuse can be overwhelming and even shaming. Some women will begin to see themselves as being foolish to have tolerated the abuse for so long. Other women may get some relief from knowing they are not alone with their experience.

2. *Be open to all specific and general examples.*
   The definitions of abuse are personalized to this group. Allow plenty of time for participants to think and reflect on what they have to contribute. Encourage members who have been silent to state their thoughts and examples. Offer to add to the definitions as new examples occur during discussion.

3. *Some women are concerned about their own abusive behavior and see their abuse as more of the problem.*
   It is important here to acknowledge that we all can be abusive on some occasions and that we must take responsibility for our own behavior. But, for now, we need to focus on what it feels like when someone abuses us and to recognize the harm that occurs when there is ongoing, systematic abuse in our relationships.

4. *Women may begin to compare their abuse to that of other women in the group.*
   One or two women may decide that their abuse isn't as bad as another woman's and conclude that they may not belong in this group. This may be said aloud, or a woman may keep these thoughts to herself. She may also be thinking of not returning to the group for this reason. If this comes out, it may be helpful to let the group respond to this issue; many members will recognize the fallacy in this thinking. You can also explain that a few choice words by an angry partner have as much potential of violating a person's rights and causing bad feelings as does a black eye. Mention that emotional abuse is very confusing because you cannot see it or touch it the way you can a broken bone or a mark on the skin.

   If this issue isn't openly stated, you may choose to say that it is common for women in groups to question whether or not this group is right for them after the first few meetings. State that those are perfectly normal thoughts and feelings. However, encourage them to stay in the group and allow themselves some time before they make a decision not to continue.

5. *Minimizing of the abuse is a common coping mechanism.*
   Ask other women in the group to address this issue when a group member states that her abuse "isn't that bad" or she is unsure if the behavior was actually abusive. The understanding and empathy of group peers can be most powerful in helping a woman to gain an understanding of the abuse occurring in her life.

6. *Confusion is an overriding experience of many battered women.*

   Explain that many reasons exist for women to feel so much confusion related to abuse. Looking at all the definitions of abuse on the chalkboard is confusing in and of itself, and a woman sometimes has to cope with being told by an abuser that she is to blame for his actions. Her children may be acting out and turning against her as well. Others in her life may be giving her conflicting advice and may have also been abusive towards her. Many times friends and family have become frustrated or angry towards her, to the point of blaming her for her partner's abuse, too. She may be totally isolated in her attempts to receive the support or encouragement she needs during her time of crisis. She has important and difficult decisions to make for herself. It is important to validate for participants that confusion is a common experience when they are being abused.

7. *The House of Abuse (4b) takes more time to complete than Defining Abuse (4a) in the four quadrants.*

   However, women relate well to the House of Abuse. It may be well worth the extra time. We suggest you experiment with both approaches.

Notes, comments, and observations:

Patterns of Abuse

Goals

In this session, participants will:

1. Better understand the dynamics of abuse and how abuse affects them.

2. Identify and talk about the pattern of abuse in their lives.

3. Understand the three stages of abuse documented by Lenore Walker in *The Cycle of Violence* and how these stages compare to their patterns of abuse.

4. Give support to group members as the patterns of abuse are shared.

Format

This session explores the patterns that have developed related to the abuse in group members' relationships. During this session, each woman will see more clearly what has been occurring in her life and how that has affected her.

1. Check-In

2. Life Patterns

Introduce this session by asking that group members close their eyes and try to relax for a few minutes. Ask them to place their feet on the floor and hands in their laps. Make gentle suggestions about draining the stress out of their bodies, starting at the tops of their heads and moving down to their feet. Allow several minutes for this while you speak softly about the stress leaving each area of the body.

Now ask them to think about some patterns in their lives. Suggest fabric patterns, textures, wall coverings, or anything that represents a repeated pattern. Allow a few minutes of silence to think about this.

Ask the women to open their eyes, and tell them you would like them to move to thinking about and visualizing the pattern of abuse in their life.

3. Patterns of Abuse

Next, provide plain paper and markers, crayons, or pastels in the middle of the circle. Explain that you would like each woman to find a place alone in the room to draw the pattern of abuse in her life as she envisioned it in the previous exercise. Quickly explain that this is not an exercise in artistic or creative ability and that anything they draw is appropriate. Stick figures, symbols, colors, and words can all be used to express their patterns.

Tell them they will have ten to fifteen minutes to draw their patterns. Ask that there be no talking during this exercise and that the room be silent until everyone has completed their patterns. Facilitators can leave the room for this time period to allow as much relaxation and quiet as possible for the group members. Return after ten minutes and announce that they have only a few more minutes to complete their pictures.

4. Sharing Pictures

When everyone has returned to the circle, explain that each woman will share her picture with the group. Tell them that the sharing is optional, but that they are strongly encouraged to do this as part of the process of talking about their abuse and beginning to heal.

Ask for a volunteer to place her picture on the floor in the middle of the circle so everyone can see it well. Have her tell about her picture, and allow time for the group members and facilitators to make observations or ask clarifying questions. It is helpful if the group asks "what, when, or how" questions rather than "why" questions, because such questions often imply blame.

Be prepared to help the woman sharing her picture with emotional responses that may occur as a result of talking about the pattern of abuse in her life. When the sharing process has been completed with the first woman, give her back her picture and ask for another volunteer.

Usually, all group members will participate in this exercise. If a member decides not to share her picture, respect that decision. You may choose to offer the woman other options. For example, you could ask if the group member would like to show her picture without an explanation, if she would share what it felt like to draw it, or if she would consider sharing it later in this or another session. This intervention respects her decision to decline sharing her picture but also allows her to consider another alternative.

Note: Sharing the patterns of abuse might take the entire session. Typically, there is not enough time remaining after completing this exercise for the time-taking portion of the group. Usually there is no break for this session because taking a break may interrupt the momentum. Announce this in advance and ask women to quietly leave and return to the room as needed on their own.

5. Cycle of Violence

If there is time remaining, it would be helpful to discuss Lenore Walker's Cycle of Violence as described in her book, *The Battered Woman Syndrome*[4]. Tell the group that Lenore Walker, a pioneer of the battered women's movement, interviewed battered women in shelters across the country in the 1970s. Then explain the cycle of violence, which she developed from her interviews.

On the chalkboard, draw the cycle of abuse (Figure A).

Figure A

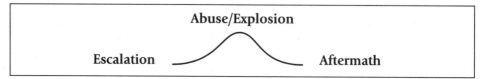

Give an example of how this might look in reality. For instance, your partner's boss criticizes him at work and he becomes more and more upset on his way home. Upon his arrival at home, he finds there is no dinner on the table. The abuse or explosion occurs (can be any of the abuses defined in last week's session), and your partner feels better. But you are now angry and upset. Draw what this looks like (Figure B).

Figure B

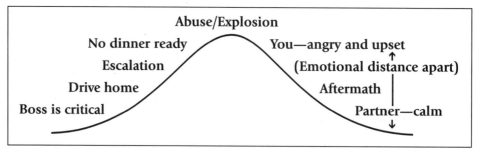

As your partner is trying to make up to you with "Let's go out for dinner" or "Let's order a pizza," chances are you will not even want to be in the same room with him, let alone want to dine at the same table. (Note: Women relate strongly to this example and can give many examples about how this happens to them.)

Another piece of this pattern is women wanting to get the abuse over with because they know it can't be avoided. During the escalation stage, they can sense and feel the abuse coming, anywhere from hours to days or even weeks in advance. Women in abusive relationships are acutely in tune with their survival instincts. They have developed many skills that have increased their chances of survival. Sometimes this has meant saving their own life or the lives of their children.

Women will often calculate the risks and determine what needs to be done immediately in order to survive. Sometimes this means that the woman may do something that she knows will trigger an abusive response from the partner so she can get the abuse over with as soon as possible. This action on her part can be anything from being assertive to name calling to a physical act. After the abusive incident, her partner will likely blame her, and she will often blame herself. He feels justified and she feels like a failure. The reality of this situation

---

[4] *Adapted from* The Battered Woman Syndrome *by Lenore Walker. Copyright 1984, Springer Publishing, New York.*

is that it is Friday night and she needs to have enough time to get past the abusive incident so that she can return to her job on Monday. Women often talk about how crazy and confusing these situations make them feel.

Next, draw how men perceive a common abusive pattern (Figure C).

Out of the blue something sets him off.

Everything is going along fine.

Everything should be forgotten and let's get back to normal.

Figure C

Explain that men are often unaware of the escalation stage and believe that their partner suddenly does something to upset them. They explode, are abusive, and then believe everything is fine again.

Last, draw how the pattern begins to look over time; for example Figure D:

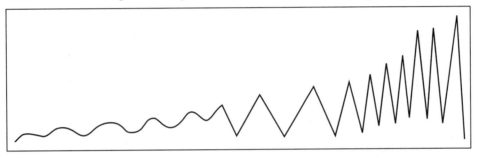

Figure D

As the abusive incidents are repeated, the incidents will often occur more frequently and become more serious. Explain that abuse actually can and does occur in all three stages of the cycle. For example, in the calming or aftermath stage (sometimes referred to as the honeymoon phase) the giving of gifts, promises, apologies, or begging for forgiveness can be a form of manipulation. This is yet another way of maintaining control and a way of causing a woman to question herself if she doesn't feel open to accepting what her partner is offering. And, in fact, he often is offering exactly what the woman has been wanting in the relationship. Yet, the only time he makes these offerings is after he has been abusive. Clearly, his motives are questionable. There may be times when he is sincere about his promises, but does not follow through on them.

Another important point to make is that some women report that there is no calming or honeymoon period or that over time the promises and gifts have disappeared. Now his behaviors display distance, emotional separation, tension, and even threats. This can be discouraging and reduces the women's hopes of the relationship ever getting better.

Conclude this activity by communicating that all the different patterns of abuse usually add up to some form of control, minimization, denial, isolation, confusion, feelings of craziness, and self-blame. Recognizing and exploring these issues and feelings will be an ongoing task for the group.

6. Closing

Issues

1. *Some group members may experience anxiety when asked to create and draw a pattern.*
   Reassure group members that this comes up in every group and that many members feel they are not artistic or creative and feel embarrassed about their drawings. Explain that no one is going to judge their picture and that simplicity is most acceptable.

2. *Some group members may feel intimidated by a very creative and artistic picture.*
   Help the group members to see that the quality of the drawing is not the issue here. What is important is how each member can express her patterns of abuse so she can see and feel what it looks like. It is always nice to applaud the creative talents of individual members while reminding the group that our gifts and talents are diverse.

3. *This is a powerful session; women may feel pain, shame, anger, sadness, grief, stress, and trauma when explaining their pattern of abuse.*
   Be prepared for the group members to have an emotional reaction to this exercise, either in talking about their own picture or in listening as other members present theirs. Allow time to explore and work through these feelings.

4. *The entire session may be needed to complete this exercise.*
   Because of the many feelings and emotions that tend to surface in this exercise, more time than usual is needed for this session. There usually is not time for individual time taking, and sometimes the group will forego the break.

5. *Walker's cycle of abuse is important information for understanding the dynamics of abuse.*
   If you are not able to present Walker's cycle in this session due to time constraints, plan to present it at the next session or as soon as possible. This information helps build a foundation of knowledge for understanding the dynamics of abuse.

6. *Self-blame will occasionally be an issue when presenting patterns of abuse.*
   This does not happen often during this exercise, but when it does, remind group members that the focus at this time is on what has been done to hurt or violate them. At this time, it is important to separate their behaviors from their partner's behaviors to get a clearer picture of the violations that have been perpetrated against them.

Notes, comments, and observations:

What Keeps Women in Abusive Relationships?

Goals:

In this session, participants will:

1. Explore the many factors that contribute to keeping women in abusive relationships.

2. Reduce shameful feelings related to staying in an abusive relationship.

3. Understand that the multiple reasons for staying must often be addressed before there is adequate strength to decide whether to stay or leave.

4. Understand that for some women staying is a safer option than leaving.

5. Accept that some women have hope that their relationship will change and improve and that this is a valid choice for any woman.

6. Recognize that society contributes to reasons that keep women in abusive relationships.

Format

This session is key to better understanding the dynamics of abuse. Most women feel relieved by finding out that there are many valid reasons for staying in abusive relationships. Hopefully, identifying what keeps group members in abusive relationships will help each group member understand better some of the decisions she has made.

1. Check-In

2. Reasons for Staying

Introduce this session by writing on the chalkboard the following sentence:

"Why do women stay in abusive relationships?"

Next, ask the group how this statement makes them feel. Tell them you are not looking for specific answers to the question, but reactions they might have to the sound of the question. The answers you will frequently hear are that it makes them feel defensive, inadequate, stupid, embarrassed, ashamed, wrong, bad, and accused. Next, ask what other question might be posed that is not being asked by most people. Write the answer:

"Why do men abuse women?" Discuss this briefly.

Finally, ask if there is a way that the question, "Why do women stay in abusive relationships?" could be rephrased. Write on the board:

"What keeps women in abusive relationships?"

This phrasing does not sound as accusatory and can be answered more readily. Ask the group members to share the actual reasons that have kept them in their abusive relationships.

This list of reasons will produce discussion and will usually take about twenty to thirty minutes to complete. If the person offering the reason appears to feel ashamed, ask for a show of hands on how many people can relate to that particular reason. A show of hands will help validate that person and help her begin to break through the shame.

Note: Ask the cofacilitator or a volunteer to record the group's list so it can be typed and handed out the following week. See Appendix B for a sample list.

3. Common Factors for Staying

When the list is complete, you typically will have twenty-five to forty reasons on the board. Ask the group members to silently count the reasons that apply to them. After a few minutes, go around the group and ask each member for her total number and write it on the board. The numbers will generally look something like this: 23, 17, 14, 21, 19, 16, 8, 15, 22, 12. Now ask the group to give their reactions to the numbers. The most common response is that they are surprised that other group members have as many reasons as they do. This helps women feel less ashamed about staying.

If there is time, discuss how society contributes to the reasons listed on the board. This is often a lively and empowering discussion.

Explain that *if* a member's goal is to leave her relationship, she will probably need to address, at some level, the reasons that keep her in the relationship. Each reason will need to be examined and resolved separately.

Tell the group that some of the most common reasons that keep group members in their abusive relationships are:

- Low self-esteem/poor self-concept
- Economic deprivation
- Witnessing violence as a child
- Keeping the family together for the sake of the children

4. Choices

Discuss the idea that three choices exist for group members in abusive relationships. They can:

- Stay and leave the relationship as it is (maintaining the status quo)
- Stay and change themselves (can't change another person)
- Leave and seek safety elsewhere (may be temporary or permanent)

The goal for all group members is to be safe and free of all forms of abuse in their relationships. How each member chooses to reach this goal is her decision and her decision alone. The group facilitators' and group members' role is to provide a safe and supportive environment in which members can feel comfortable and confident in making their own decisions about their lives.

Break

5. Individual Time Taking

6. Closing

Issues

1. *This is a significant session because group members often feel confused and ashamed for staying in an abusive relationship.*
   Take every opportunity to validate group members for current decisions about staying or leaving, and remind them that there are many legitimate reasons for staying. Shame is an issue for most group members who choose to stay in an abusive relationship and for those who have left but question why they stayed as long as they did. Reduce shame by consistently pointing out the number of women who relate to any particular reason for staying. "You are not alone" is often a much-needed message for group members. Also acknowledge how extremely difficult it is for a member to leave an abusive relationship, given the number of factors involved.

2. *The list of reasons for staying in an abusive relationship can represent new and helpful information or information that can be discouraging for some group members.*
   Group members have many different responses to this session. They may feel relieved, not so alone, better informed, or they may feel emotionally stressed at the complexity of why they stay. Be prepared for a wide range of feelings, emotions, and thoughts about this exercise.

3. *Group members may decide to give a member advice on what she should do.*
   Giving advice can be problematic. See our discussion of giving advice on page 15. Ask the woman if advice is helpful for her to hear. Ask carefully and tactfully to avoid shaming the advice giver. Remind the group that each woman has her own answers and timing for her particular situation. We believe that the facilitators should not in any way suggest or force the issue

of whether or not a woman should leave her abusive partner. *It is always appropriate, though, to tell a member that you are concerned for her safety and want to be sure she has a plan in place, if needed.*

Notes, comments, and observations:

Emotional Abuse

Goals

In this session, participants will:

1. Define emotional abuse.

2. Understand the confusion that is caused by emotional abuse.

3. Become aware of the emotional abuse in their own lives.

4. Understand the effects of emotional abuse.

5. Identify a plan for reversing the damage to self-esteem caused by emotional abuse.

Format

Emotional abuse, as addressed in this session, is a separate topic from other types of abuse because of the extreme impact it has on women. Emotional abuse is more covert than some other forms of abuse. Therefore understanding its damage is more difficult.

1. Check-In

2. Emotional Abuse Defined

Introduce this topic by discussing why we dedicate a whole session to just one type of abuse. Points you might discuss include:

- Emotional abuse is considered by many to be the worst kind of abuse

- Emotional abuse is the most difficult to identify

- Emotional abuse has the longest-lasting effect

Suggest that perhaps all other types of abuse (physical, sexual, verbal) are forms of emotional abuse. Give the following example to illustrate this point.

> Five years ago a woman slipped on the ice and broke her arm. Medical treatment was secured and her arm healed successfully. In that same time period, her partner assaulted her and broke her other arm. Again, her arm was treated and the healing process was successful.

Which broken arm causes her pain and hurtful memories today? Discuss.

Maybe it's possible, though, that physical abuse doesn't hurt our feelings in quite the same way as words/emotional abuse does. Illustrate with the following:

> An abused woman told the story of her partner physically assaulting her so severely that she had to be taken by ambulance to the hospital. Her partner disappeared before the ambulance and police arrived. As she was being carried out of their home on a stretcher, her partner reappeared and yelled at the police in apparent shock and anger, "Who did this horrible thing to my wife? I'm going to find that S.O.B. and kill him." She was crushed by his denial of what he had done to her. His words hurt her far beyond the physical pain she experienced.

As these examples show, emotional abuse can be confusing. Emotional abuse is real, harmful, and leaves scars that usually can't be seen but last a long time.

Help the group define emotional abuse. Write the group's ideas on the board and add any of the following to help with the definition:

- A breaking of the spirit of another person
- An attack on a person's self-worth
- Controlling another person by manipulating that person's feelings
- Systematic and ongoing harsh verbal treatment

3. Emotional Abuse in Our Own Lives

Talk about emotional abuse being a widespread problem that is difficult to identify and understand. It is a subtle form of abuse with no obvious wounds. The scars of emotional abuse are hidden and are an attack on the spirit. Ask the group if they can relate to this information about emotional abuse. Ask some of the following questions:

- Does your partner's anger scare you?
- Is *not* making your partner angry a frequent goal of yours?
- Do you suffer more than is necessary in your relationship?
- Are you suspicious of your partner's kindness?
- Do you feel more as if you have a parent than a partner?
- Do you often feel as if you're walking on eggshells?

Copy and pass out the Emotional Abuse Checklist worksheet in Appendix G. Give the group a few minutes to fill this out. When it's completed, go around the circle and ask each woman to comment on how she related to this checklist and whether she could see a pattern of emotional abuse in her life. Ask if she can identify examples of emotional abuse that were not included in this list.

4. Effects of Emotional Abuse

Next, talk about what happens to victims of emotional abuse or what the potential results of being emotionally abused are. Write the group's ideas plus any of the following on the chalkboard:

• Low self-esteem   • Suicidal thoughts • Lack of self-worth   • Shyness • Difficulty taking risks   • Developmental problems • Problems with relationships   • Feelings of incompetence • Withdrawal from people; isolation   • Feeling fatigued

Suggest that emotional abuse implies that you are not a good person and that you deserve to be hurt. Emotional abuse also encourages dependency.

Talk about the psychological needs that are critical for a person's well-being. Write on the chalkboard:

• Sense of being worthwhile • Need for feeling and giving love

Emotional abuse is an attack on these needs and is destructive to a person's functioning. These two psychological needs are important for all people. It is important to recognize when these needs are being thwarted or damaged and to find a way to reverse this course.

5. Action Plan

Ask the group how they might go about taking some action to stop or reverse some of the damage of emotional abuse. Ideas for this might include:

- A self-esteem support group
- Reading about women and self-esteem
- Writing in your journal
- Building a more supportive network
- Avoiding people who are harmful to your esteem
- Avoiding negative self-talk
- Letting go of the desire to change others
- Reestablishing positive relationships you enjoyed in the past

Ask each group member to identify two ways she can enhance her self-esteem. Ask for a specific time period when this plan can be put into action. Ask each woman to explain her plan.

Break

6. Individual Time Taking

7. Closing

Issues

1. *Emotional abuse can be difficult for group members to understand.*
   Sometimes women are so accustomed to put-downs and attacks on their self-esteem that they have little or no recognition of how these attacks might be harmful to them. It feels like a normal way of life. Some group members may doubt that the effects of emotional abuse are real; they may blame themselves for the negative behavior of a partner or another person. They may think they deserve this kind of maltreatment. Be prepared to talk about society's role in allowing attacks on women.

2. *List and discuss specific examples of emotional abuse in this session, if desired.*
   It may or may not be necessary to repeat information on identifying specific types of abuse. However, a quick review may be helpful at the beginning of the session. Include examples covered in the second session, such as ways that abusive partners ignore, control, ridicule, insult, humiliate, harass, and manipulate their partners.

3. *Use concrete examples of emotional abuse to help group members understand it better.*
   Over time, group facilitators have heard many stories of emotional abuse. You may want to share stories you think make good examples of how emotional abuse is perpetrated.

4. *Emotional abuse leads to hurt and anger.*
   Most women are socialized to avoid anger and to present themselves as sweet and nice. Consequently, feelings of hurt and anger have often been ignored or avoided for much of a woman's lifetime. This session may cause some hurt and anger to surface, often unexpectedly. Allow time to discuss emotions that may arise. Addressing emotional abuse can be powerful and even frightening for some group members.

5. *Emotional abuse is not an occasional lashing out or a one-time event.*
   Group facilitators should be aware of the systematic, ongoing, and intentional nature of emotional abuse. Erosion of self-esteem occurs over time, not overnight. If a woman is exposed long enough to someone's negative behavior and words, she will likely begin to believe what is said, causing her to withdraw or isolate herself.

6. *More subtle forms of emotional abuse can be difficult to identify.*
Because some group members have never been called a name or had a threat made against them, they may believe that emotional abuse is not occurring and that they are the one with the problem. This simply is not true.

A woman can be severely emotionally abused by a more covert type of behavior on the part of her partner. Examples include: emotional withdrawal; sabotaging her efforts; lying or cheating; maintaining power and control over money; expecting her to always ask for permission to go places; or expecting her to express constant gratitude for what he does for her.

The list goes on and on. Some partners are very good at communicating disapproval and dislike without ever calling a woman a name or threatening her. It is important to be aware of the more subtle forms of abuse and the damage caused to the spirit.

Notes, comments, and observations:

Anger about Abuse

Goals

In this session, participants will:

1. Learn that anger is an acceptable and appropriate feeling that is important to a woman's well-being.
2. Learn what to do with anger when it is identified.
3. Address their anger towards a specific person.
4. Find creative ways to express anger that are safe for themselves and others.

Format

Women in general seem to have a great deal of anger that they have never been given permission to express. Women who have been abused *always* have anger about the abuse, whether or not they have identified that anger. This session will help members identify their anger about abuse and learn ways to express that anger.

1. Check-In

Ask participants to share briefly a situation in which they were angry during the past week.

2. Girls, Women, and Anger

Begin this session with a general discussion of how women have historically felt about anger. Talk about what women were taught about anger as young girls and how that has affected their adult lives. Include the idea that, as women, we have often been taught to conform and not ask questions. Ask if anyone associates the label "bitch" with anger.

Introduce the idea that depression may be related to unexpressed anger, and the potentially harmful effects this may have on both physical and emotional well-being. Ask how they think men and women differ in the ways they respond to anger. Last, talk about anger as a normal and appropriate feeling that often masks other feelings, such as fear, sadness, and betrayal.

3. Identifying Anger

On the chalkboard, write:

What to do with anger?

1. Acknowledge it
2. Find the feeling underneath it
3. Allow it—feel it in your body
4. Act on it—choose a way to express it appropriately

Briefly discuss these four points as well as the importance of acknowledging anger in appropriate ways in the future.

4. Anger Letter Exercise

This exercise involves writing a letter to someone with whom participants are angry. Preferably, it will be the abusive partner or ex-partner in their lives, but it can be anyone with whom they are angry.

Communicate that this letter is *not* intended to be given or sent to the abusive person. Instead, it is intended as a way for women to identify and express their anger in a healthy manner. The letter can be of any length; any language they wish to use is appropriate; the composition, spelling, and grammar are unimportant and will not be judged.

Allow fifteen minutes for group members to write their letters. Leaders can leave the room for this time. When the fifteen-minute period is up, some women will still be writing. Gently request that the letters be completed within the next few minutes. When everyone is ready, do an informal check-in on how it felt to write a letter expressing anger. Be careful not to get involved in a specific person's anger at this time.

Next, tell the group that you would like to have each person read her letter to the group. As always, this is optional for each participant, but is highly encouraged as an important part of the process of dealing with anger. Ask for a volunteer to start. After she has completed reading her letter, ask the group members for comments, observations, or support they can give the person. Allow ample time for each woman to receive feedback and support. As the letters are read to the group, members who were initially reluctant to share their letters will often change their minds and decide to read what they wrote.

After the reading and feedback are finished, tell the group that they have choices about what to do with their letters. They can give them to the group leader to keep, they can destroy them (provide a wastebasket), or they can keep them for future reference. Usually, women want to rid themselves of their anger letters.

Ask each woman to comment on what it was like to participate in this exercise. It is important to point out how uncomfortable we, as women, are with our anger. Writing the letter, reading the letter, and feeling the angry feelings may have been fairly difficult for many of the group members. Other group members may feel exhilarated by this opportunity.

To conclude this session, take a few minutes to think of appropriate ways to respond to one's anger. These ideas can be ridiculous and irrational as long as no one is harmed. This list might include writing in a journal, talking to someone, throwing things, screaming alone, or having private temper tantrums.

Break (if time allows)

5. Individual Time Taking (if time allows)

6. Closing

At the end of this session, introduce the "Most Hurtful Incident" topic so women can prepare for the next group meeting. Explain that this is an opportunity for each woman to talk about her personal experience of being abused. It is important to tell the group that there is no right or wrong way to talk about this and that women from other groups have chosen many different ways of doing it. See the next session for additional information.

Issues

1. *Time is almost always a factor for this session.*
   This topic cannot be rushed and often takes all of the session time to complete. The group may be willing to forego the break or the individual time taking in this session.

2. *Emotional responses to anger letters can be difficult and frightening for both the reader of the letter and other group members.*
   Post-traumatic stress symptoms and flashbacks may occasionally occur during this session. Be prepared to work through these stresses as they arise for group members. When this happens, be prepared to support the group member having the flashback. Sometimes a facilitator will sit by the member and comfort her. One facilitator might leave the room with her if she needs time away from the group.

3. *Some group members are concerned that the language and words they want to use might offend other group members.*
   Encourage them to use whatever words are needed, and ask the group members to be understanding and nonjudgmental about such language.

4. *Expressing anger may be a frightening exercise for some group members because the concept is foreign to them and because showing anger is typically unsafe for them to do.*
   When introducing this exercise, encourage group members to remember that this is a safe place to express anger, without fearing judgment and

shame. Stress the importance of expressing anger as a human right and as a good and appropriate thing to do.

5. *Occasionally, a group member will choose to write to herself as the person with whom she is the most angry.*
This is not expected by the group and needs to be handled with caution by the facilitator. Validate the person but also encourage her to look at possible needless self-blame.

6. *Some group members will begin reading their letters and then find themselves unable to complete the reading due to the feelings that arise.*
Know how difficult this exercise can be and offer the group member reading her letter time to work through her feelings and resume sharing her letter. If this is not possible for her, ask if she would like someone else to read her letter. You may need to come back to this group member after everyone else has shared their letters.

7. *If a group member has difficulty with reading or writing and cannot write her own letter, a facilitator can offer to write the letter for her and read it as well.*
Do this only with the member's permission.

8. *Don't underestimate the power of this session or the time needed to successfully complete it.*
This session can be very draining for the facilitator as well as the group members. Offering support throughout this session requires a significant amount of compassion and empathy. Be prepared to care for yourself.

9. *Each group member knows her own safety level related to expressing her anger to an abusive person.*
Make it clear that group members are not being encouraged to express their anger in an unsafe setting. This letter is *not* meant to stimulate women to take immediate action and to express their anger toward an abusive partner at this time. Instead, the exercise is designed to help women become aware of their anger and understand that they have the right to feel the way they do.

Notes, comments, and observations:

Cluster 2

Understanding the Impact of Abuse

Most Hurtful Incident

Goals

In this session, participants will:

1. Express to the group their personal abuse experiences.

2. Describe a situation that has been particularly hurtful to them (related to their abuse).

3. Break the silence about incidents of abuse that have been difficult to discuss.

4. Continue the healing process in their journey of understanding abuse and its impact.

5. Listen to the stories of group peers to understand that no person is alone in being abused.

6. Accept support, encouragement, and feedback from the group.

7. Be aware of the need to care for themselves after group and during the week.

Format

In this session, women are being asked to tell about a "most hurtful incident" that has been perpetrated against them in their abusive relationship. This is an opportunity for a woman to share with the group the parts of her abuse story or a particular incident that she wants the group to hear and know about. By "most hurtful incident," we mean any type of abuse. For example, women often share that the abuse which has affected them most was something said to them rather than a physically violent act. This sharing will cover the next several weeks of group, as each woman is given a block of time to do this.

1. Check-In

2. Define Hurtful Incidents—Why Talk about Them?

Introduce this activity to the group by explaining that for the next several weeks the format of each session will change from an educational topic to one called "most hurtful incident." (Note: Start this process at the end of the previous session so the group members are not surprised or caught off-guard by this change in the format. Advance notice also allows them to prepare for this session.)

Explain that this is an opportunity for each woman to talk about her personal experience related to being abused. Tell the group that there is no right or wrong way to talk about their most hurtful incident and that women from other groups have chosen different ways of doing it. At this point, anxiety may increase for the group members, so find ways to alleviate the anxiety as quickly as possible.

Acknowledge that you know this probably sounds scary but that past groups have found it to be a positive and healing experience. Remind them that all activities in this group are optional, but that every woman will be encouraged to participate in this activity.

A most hurtful incident is an incident of abuse that stands out in a woman's mind. It can be any kind of abuse (physical, verbal, sexual, or emotional) and very often is something that was said to her by her partner. The facilitators should provide examples for the group.

Women choose a variety of ways to approach talking about their personal abuse experience. Many women want to tell about their history of abuse in a chronological manner. This is perfectly acceptable, but as the facilitator you may want to help them focus on a most hurtful incident at the end of their story. Some women will think about and prepare what they are going to say for days and weeks in advance. Others will spontaneously tell their story in group. Some women will write their story out and read it to the group. Others will have notes to jog their memory. Some women will bring pictures or other visual aids to share with the group while talking. Whatever way each woman approaches the activity is okay, but each woman should focus on a most hurtful incident or isolated incident at some point in her story.

Next, ask the group what they think might be the purpose of doing this activity for the next several weeks. On the chalkboard write what they say along with the following reasons:

- To acknowledge that the abuse has occurred
- To give them the right to feel as they do
- To provide a safe place to break the silence
- To be a part of the healing process and have a chance to move forward
- To feel supported and understood

Finally, ask if anyone has any questions or comments. Tell them that this activity will take the next five or six group sessions; approximately two women will tell their story and most hurtful incident each week.

The structure of the sessions will be as follows:

a) Select a first volunteer.

b) Allow twenty to thirty minutes for the group member to talk about her abuse story and "most hurtful incident." Tell her she will be able to do this without interruption. When she is finished, ask the group if they have any comments, questions, observations, or encouragement they'd like to offer.

c) Make therapeutic interventions as necessary. Assure the woman that she's not crazy or responsible for the abuse.

d) After the feedback process is completed, ask the woman what it was like for her to tell her story and most hurtful incident. Responses will vary from feeling scared, to relief, to feeling better, to indifference. Allow for thirty to forty minutes per woman for the entire process.

e) Repeat the process with the next volunteer.

Break

3. Individual Time Taking

4. Closing

Ask group members to share something they plan to do to take care of themselves after group and during the week.

Note: Ask for two or three volunteers for the next session at the end of group.

Issues

1. *This exercise may cause some anxiety-based responses.*
   Address anxiety by quickly assuring women that there is no right or wrong way of doing this exercise and that, of course, it is optional. If a member is particularly anxious, you may suggest that she wait until other women have completed this exercise to give herself some time and space to feel comfortable about participating in it. Also, each woman will be supported through the process by her group peers and the facilitators.

2. *Be aware of how powerful this activity can be for the group member telling her story.*
   This activity has the potential of bringing up memories of the abuse that can cause flashbacks and post-traumatic stress symptoms. As the facilitator, be prepared to help work through a woman's reaction. This might include changing chairs with another group member so that you can sit next to her. You might also ask if she would like you to hold her hand or touch her on the arm or shoulder to comfort her in this process.

3. *Be aware, also, of how powerful this activity can be for the group members who are listening to another member's story.*
Some women will have an emotional response that causes them to silently cry or emote in other ways. Acknowledge how the story must have touched something similar that they have experienced and allow them a chance to share their feelings, as appropriate.

4. *Occasionally, a group member will only have a few words to say about her abuse.*
As a facilitator, you may have to ask a few key questions, probe for a little more information, and help some group members along with the process. A woman may be minimizing the abuse or experiencing some denial around it. She may be fearful of feelings it could bring up.

5. *Sometimes group members avoid their feelings and can only talk about their abuse on a cognitive level.*
It is important to try to help group members move from their heads to their hearts. Ask them what it would be like to let themselves feel their sadness or hurt. Hand out the Feeling Vocabulary sheet in Appendix C to help them identify what they might be feeling.

6. *These sessions are usually stressful for everyone.*
Remind the group that this can be an emotional and difficult process for many group members and that they may have reactions even after they have left for home. Some women may experience a delayed response later in the week. Some women will find themselves dreaming about the abusive stories. Emphasize that group members may react at different times and need to find positive ways to care for themselves outside of the group.

7. *Talk with the members about ways to nurture themselves after group.*
Women usually suggest things like warm baths, soft music, candles, a good book, and hot tea as ways to care for themselves after group. Of course, some women can't even consider these options, so you'll need to help them create something else that will work for them after the group is over. Suggest visiting or calling a friend. Encourage them to use their support systems whenever possible. Remind them that writing in their journals may be an excellent way to address feelings. You may want to suggest they call and check in with you during the week.

8. *Look for ways to care for yourself.*
The abuse you hear about as a facilitator in these sessions may be difficult to handle. Sometimes you may feel like a secondary victim. If you find it difficult to leave the stress of your work experience behind at the end of the session, you may need to seek extra support and care for yourself. Discuss your feelings with your cofacilitator if at all possible. Seek out a colleague or use a staff meeting to work through your feelings. Remember what the group members suggest—hot tea, candles, music, bubble baths. Losing yourself in a good book, writing in a journal, or taking a brisk walk can be stress relievers for you also.

Notes, comments, and observations:

Impact of Negative Messages

Goals

In this session, participants will:

1. Examine the negative messages women have heard.

2. Recognize the impact of negative messages on women.

3. Become aware of how women internalize and accept negative messages.

4. Reject negative messages and rewrite them into positive messages.

Format

In this session, group members explore the many negative messages they have heard and internalized over time. They then learn ways to reject those messages, replacing them with self-affirming ideas.

1. Check-In

2. Negative Messages

Tell the group that at this session they will be talking about "who we are as women" in relation to the messages women have heard and integrated. They will be looking at (write on the chalkboard):

> *How messages of the past have affected women's:*
> - Self-esteem
> - Self-image
> - Chosen goals
> - Relationship choices

Ask the group to think about where and from whom they might have heard these messages. Write on the chalkboard:

> As a woman, and as a girl, I have heard negative messages from:

Responses you can expect to hear include:

- Parents
- Grandparents
- Peers
- Siblings
- Friends
- Partners
- Teachers
- Employers
- Advertisers
- Neighbors
- Authority figures
- Clergy
- Men

Next, ask the group to think about messages they have heard that have negatively affected them in some way. Messages can be from any period in their lives. Start this exercise with an example like being told, "Who do you think you are?"

Some examples of responses you might hear are:

- Stop that crying, or I'll really give you something to cry about.
- You'll never amount to anything.
- You think you know everything.
- You're a bitch—just like all the rest of them.
- Children should be seen and not heard.
- Why can't you be like your brother?
- You're so emotional!
- I wish you'd never been born.
- You'll never find a man the way you look.
- She's only a housewife.
- Girls can't do that!

This list can be lengthy as the group members begin to remember things that were said to them. Memories seem to be triggered by other women's negative messages. Many of the messages are graphic and personal to the individual group member. Messages may have negative sexual, racial, appearance, and gender overtones.

3. How We Internalize Negative Messages

When the list on the chalkboard has been completed, give each member an opportunity to say how she feels. Ask group members to comment on how these messages may have affected their self-esteem, the goals they have chosen, or the relationships they are in. Communicate to the group that boys hear some of these same messages as well, and that the impact on them can be equally devastating.

4. Rejecting Negative Messages

Discuss with the group that women do important work that is frequently not valued or reimbursed and that sometimes women are not valued as worthwhile beings. Tell them change starts with each of us as individuals and that we can begin to value ourselves as women. One of the ways to do that is to change and rewrite the negative messages we have heard and believed.

Look at the messages on the chalkboard and ask the group members to turn them into positive messages. Examples might be:

- Who do you think you are? **I am someone, I am important**.
- You think you know everything. **I know a great deal and I'm learning more every day**.
- You're so emotional! **I'm glad I have feelings. My feelings help me sort things out**.
- You're a bitch—just like all the rest of them. **I'm assertive and unique. I'm human and humans have feelings**.

Suggest to the group that they can deflect negative messages and refuse to allow them to become a part of their beings. This is not an easy task, but with some careful thought it can be accomplished.

5. Acknowledging Personal Negative Messages

Finally, distribute small slips of paper to the group and ask the members to write down negative messages or words that they would like to never have to hear again. Suggest they use a separate slip of paper for each message, and allow five minutes to do this. Place a wastebasket in the center of the group. Ask for a volunteer to read her messages aloud, tear them up, and throw them away. Then each group member in turn will read her messages aloud. Write on the chalkboard:

> - These words do not belong to me.
> - These words are not who I am.

Tell group members they can say these sentences, if they choose to, after discarding their negative messages.

> **Break**

6. Individual Time Taking

7. Closing

Read a handout or poem on self-esteem.

Issues

1. *A common bond occurs for group members as they acknowledge the negative messages they have heard.*
   Reinforcing this common experience can help to reduce shame and embarrassment. It feels good for group members to know they are not alone with negative messages that have been said to them by people who are supposed to care about them.

2. *Powerful emotions such as sadness, hurt, humiliation, and anger may occur as members read their personal negative messages.*
   Prepare yourself and the group for these potential feelings. Allow time to process these feelings.

3. *Remind group members that these messages will not necessarily go away just because they wrote them down and acknowledged them.*
   Suggest that the messages or words may not be as powerful for them when they hear them again. Encourage mentally deflecting negative words back to the person saying them rather than internalizing these words.

4. *Rewriting negative messages into positive messages can be difficult initially until women gain practice.*
   Encourage women to practice turning negative messages to positive ones. Suggest getting the help of a trusted friend to find new ways to rewrite these words.

Notes, comments, and observations:

Common Experiences of Battered Women

Goals

In this session, participants will:

1. List and explore the common experiences that occur for battered women.

2. Identify the issues that are a part of each woman's experience.

3. Discuss how to begin solving these problems.

4. Acknowledge how much energy a battered woman uses on a daily basis to deal with the stresses of these issues.

Format

Women who are abused have many experiences in common, a fact that has become apparent in the group over the past several weeks. This session will explore some of the many commonalities that are so painful for women who have been abused.

1. Check-In

2. Common Issues

Begin the session by talking about the many different kinds of negative effects that can occur for women who are battered. These common experiences or issues may occur infrequently, occasionally, or fairly often.

The abuse and the results of these experiences can make daily life very difficult for a battered woman because she needs to be vigilant about potential abuse. To avoid the negative impact of these experiences, she often must avoid the abuse. This takes a tremendous toll on her available energy.

On the chalkboard, write the following issues for battered women:

• Trauma	• Confusion	• Post-traumatic
• Fear/terror	• Isolation	stress symptoms
• Shame	• Depression	• Grief and loss
• Anger/rage	• Minimization	
• Fear of loneliness	• Sadness	

Communicate that this is not a comprehensive list of issues, but that these are twelve key issues to which many battered women can relate.

Next, talk about and expand on each issue individually. Write the comments on the board as you discuss the issues. Be prepared to offer explanations and give examples of how each issue affects battered women. Ask the cofacilitator or a group member to record the group's thoughts on each issue for later distribution.

Trauma

Battered women can experience both physical and emotional trauma. They may experience an unexpected or sudden physical assault that is traumatizing, or an emotional attack that is jarring to their psychological well-being.

Examples of severe abuse that can cause trauma are:

- Having a loaded revolver held to your head while the abuser plays Russian roulette.

- Having your locked door broken down, a gun placed to your head, and the trigger pulled while your children watch.

- Having your children told to say good-bye to you, "because the next time they'd see you would be in the cemetery."

While not all battered women feel traumatized, it is an issue that is very difficult for those who do.

Fear/Terror

Being fearful can become a way of life for a battered woman. She may need to be constantly on guard and on the lookout for what is going to happen next. It may be difficult for her to accomplish ordinary and routine tasks due to ongoing feelings of fear. Threats are often part of a battered woman's experience and these can terrify her. Fear and terror are manifested in many different ways for battered women and can be overt or covert.

Shame

Battered women usually feel shame about the abuse in some way, as at some level they believe they should be able to control or prevent it. It seems that the great majority of victims of violent and abusive acts feel some degree of responsibility for the abuse. This is particularly true of partner abuse because women are so often held responsible in our culture for making relationships work. Since shame becomes such an integral part of our being, battered women often see themselves as bad or negative people who are not worthwhile.

Anger/Rage

Battered women are angry and sometimes full of rage at their abusive partners. They can also be angry at themselves for whatever they perceive they have done to "allow the abuse." Since anger is basically an unbecoming or suspicious label for women, they will frequently try to prevent their anger from showing. If they express their anger or rage, they often see themselves in a negative light.

The system is suspicious of a woman who is described as angry. The implication is that a woman who is angry is at fault for what is happening in the relationship.

Anger can be a difficult, lose-lose issue for women. If it is expressed, the woman looks bad. If it is ignored or suppressed, she experiences many other harmful consequences.

Fear of Loneliness

Undoubtedly, the fear of loneliness has to be one of the greatest human fears. It looms large for battered women. Many battered women have a difficult time imagining themselves alone and without a partner. They are often so fused to their partner(s) that they can see no other way of life. Tolerating and working around the abuse is far easier for them than the thought of being alone.

Women are socialized to be half of a relationship. They grow up listening to songs like, "Stand By Your Man" and "You're Nobody 'Til Somebody Loves You." Messages like these have a powerful impact on a woman's identity, and being alone is not a part of who she ever had planned to be. Being alone, or the thought of being alone, can strike a paralyzing core of fear in a woman. The fear of being alone is an often-discussed reason that keeps women in their relationships.

Confusion

Almost all battered women talk about the confusion they feel. Confusion is almost inevitable in an abusive relationship.

Battered women have significant issues about whether or not they are crazy. They feel crazy and abusive partners tell them they are crazy. This causes confusion for the battered woman. No one is telling her that she's *not* crazy. Most people in her life don't understand what's happening to her or her confusion about the relationship. She often will blame herself for either getting into or not getting out of her situation and cannot explain it to others or even to herself.

A battered woman has a great deal to sort out. She has many important and difficult decisions to make. She may be getting conflicting advice from different people. She is trying to figure out what is causing the abuse. At the very least, she feels confused about how much responsibility she has for the abuse and about the many messages she is getting.

Isolation

Isolation is an all-too-common experience for battered women and it comes about ever so subtly. It contributes to a downward spiral of a woman's self-esteem because she has limited or no interaction to validate her worth as a person. Most battered women relate to and understand this experience and can explain how and when it began.

Isolation often occurs as a result of the man making disparaging remarks about her family and choice of friends. This is followed by a request and later a demand that she stop interacting with them. Often, she views agreeing to this demand as a sacrifice on her part to make their relationship better and stronger. At the same time, the man often continues to see whoever he pleases.

One woman told about her partner announcing a few days after their wedding that for the first six months of their marriage they would not be seeing anyone else except each other. Though this caused some anxiety for her, she thought that she could ignore it and it would go away. Within days of the honeymoon, he was telling her where she could and couldn't go, and the isolation from friends and family had begun.

Many factors appear to contribute to isolation. A lack of transportation or telephone access plays a significant role. Other factors include no supportive family living in the area; being made to leave the work force; not having access to financial resources; and having one's activity monitored. Women who have partners in the military are often uprooted from their friends, families, and familiar social or work environments. Other women face similar situations when asked to give up some things to follow their partner's career or desires. Women who live in rural areas often are very isolated from resources.

Depression

Depression and abuse go hand in hand for many battered women. Battered women experience having someone else hold power and control over them, which usually results in feeling oppressed. Oppression and depression may also go hand in hand.

Battered women are not as free to move around in the world as nonabused women. They often have restrictions on their activity, behavior, thoughts, and even emotions. This can cause feelings of hopelessness, disruption of thinking, sadness, sleeping and eating disturbances, and inactivity. These symptoms are frequently associated with depression.

Many battered women identify themselves as depressed and are getting some kind of help for depression, including medication. They often feel ashamed about being depressed and will not openly discuss this until they become aware that they are not alone with their depression.

Minimization

Minimization is a common characteristic or defense mechanism for battered women. If a woman can convince herself that things are "not that bad," she can live with the abuse more easily.

Frequently, women will minimize abuse by comparing their abuse to another woman's. Since a woman can always find someone whose abuse is more severe or physically damaging than hers, she is often in the position of believing that she is making something out of nothing or a mountain out of a molehill. Another means of minimization is to believe that since past threats have not been carried out, they won't be acted upon in the future. This may or may not be true.

She may also receive messages from trusted friends and family that "it's not that bad" or that she should be "thankful for all the good things you possess" (home, car, his income). Women have talked about turning to professionals such as clergy, doctors, or counselors who have given them messages like "count your blessings" or "you're overly sensitive" or "just try a little harder." The woman gets a clear message that she has something to do with ending or controlling the abuse.

Minimizing comes in many sizes and shapes and can be a dangerous way of dealing with abuse. It is difficult for some women to look at the reality of their abusive experience; minimizing the abuse helps them avoid reality.

Sadness

Being abused in any number of ways causes many women to feel sad. This sadness often overwhelms them and wears away at their self-esteem. They can barely talk about the abuse without tearing up or crying. They look sad and are unaware of how sad they really are. The sadness they feel often prevents them from getting angry about the abuse and they sometimes have difficulty taking action to protect themselves.

Women who experience significant sadness often feel a need to protect the abuser. They are concerned about his emotional or physical well-being and afraid that he may fall apart or possibly commit suicide if she leaves. He may have threatened this in the past and may even have shown past signs of such behaviors. They are frequently forgiving of him at times that may be inappropriate for their own emotional or physical safety.

Post-Traumatic Stress Symptoms

Post-traumatic stress is a reaction to an experience outside the range of normal. It is often associated with the reactions of combat veterans. It is also associated with the reactions of battered women.

Some abuse causes women to have a post-traumatic stress reaction. The severity of the abuse is not necessarily the key to why this reaction occurs. The key is more the effect of the abuse and how it feels like having been through combat. Women with post-traumatic stress symptoms will often experience flashbacks; talking about the abuse will place them back on the front line (or in the abusive incident).

Post-traumatic stress is accompanied by feelings of hopelessness, loss of self-esteem, psychic numbing, memory loss, anxiety attacks, and frequent illness. Battered women should be aware of possible post-traumatic stress symptoms so they do not feel they are crazy.

Grief and Loss

Grief is a normal response when there has been a loss of some kind. For battered women, the loss is often the dream of the relationship and a happy future in that relationship.

The abused woman may experience multiple losses at the same time. She may be losing her sense of self while losing her partner's good will towards her. Along with this may come concrete losses—home, financial security, job, custody of children, friends, and personal items of value to her. While all this confusion is occurring, finding time and space to grieve may be impossible.

Sometimes the grieving process has to be delayed while more immediate problems are attended to. It is helpful for battered women to understand this and to be aware that they may need to grieve for their losses at a later date.

3. Issues and Solutions

When the discussion is over, ask the group members to identify one or two issues they feel are a part of their abuse experience. Go around the group again and ask for one or two ideas on how they have solved these issues or plan to begin finding solutions for them.

Break

4. Individual Time Taking

5. Closing

Issues

1. *Discussing twelve issues is time consuming.*
   It is important to figure out the timing for this session and keep the group moving. Group members are likely to want to share examples of their experience. This is encouraged, but you'll need to set limits in an attempt to stay on track.

2. *Some women will have experienced most or all of these issues.*
   Women may become overwhelmed or distraught when they see so many issues all at once. Be prepared to work through this with individual women if needed.

3. *It can be affirming for women to see the negative impact of all these issues.*
   Some women feel better when they understand how common their experiences are because this reduces their feelings of being "crazy." They can see how anyone might feel overwhelmed or "crazy" when there are so many things occurring for them simultaneously.

Notes, comments, and observations:

Impact of Abuse on Children

Goals

In this session, participants will:

1. Recognize how children experience confusion related to the abuse of their mother and how their confusion is often similar to an abused woman's.
2. Identify factors that contribute to the impact of abuse on children.
3. Understand the key issues for children in violent homes.
4. Process ideas on the needs of children living in violent homes.
5. Experience feelings that group members had as children in their family-of-origin settings.

Format

Women have strong feelings about seeing their children being affected by abuse in the home. Consequently, they will often try to keep the abuse hidden. It seems, though, that no matter what a woman does to try to protect her children, kids know and often blame themselves for the abuse that is happening to their mother. This session will look at the experience of the child in an abusive home.

1. Check-In

2. Confusion and Children

Begin this session by talking about how abuse can be confusing for children in many of the same ways that it confuses women who are abused. Ask the members to think about the many times confusion has been mentioned and discussed in this group. Suggest that they think of their children's confusion in some of the same ways as they see their own.

Communicate that abuse has a very confusing effect on children. Explain that two things are occurring simultaneously for children. They are being traumatized at some level while witnessing or listening to abuse towards their mother. At the same time, they are learning that people can get their way through the use of power and control. The following poem is an example of the confusion that children feel. Read this poem to the group and take time to discuss the group's response.

> My Daddy is a monster.
> He hurts my mommy.
> He hurts me too.
> Sometimes he hits.
> Sometimes he says things
> That scare me and
> Make my mommy cry.
> After he leaves
> Sometimes I wish he
> Won't come back . . . ever.
> I love my daddy.[5]

Communicate that there are many factors to be considered when thinking of the impact of abuse on children. Ask the group to think about what they have observed in their own children or what they remember in their own childhood experience related to abuse. Ask the group what they think about children learning these two messages at the same time. Ask for examples of this from their personal experience with their children or themselves.

3. Impact of Abuse on Children

Next, ask the group to brainstorm ways children might be affected by abuse. Expect to hear some of the following and write them on the chalkboard:

- Hidden scars
- Ongoing tension in the home
- Mixed emotions about both parents
- Taking on adult responsibilities
- Becoming part of a conspiracy of silence
- Waiting for abuse to happen again
- Sleep disruption
- Poor nutrition
- Concentration problems or behavior problems at school
- Depression and anxiety
- Feelings of abandonment
- Self-blame
- Fear of mom being hurt

- Acting-out behaviors
- Withdrawal into self; isolation
- Regression to bed wetting, thumb sucking
- Trying to be perfect; causing no problems
- Low self-esteem
- Using violence to solve problems
- Feelings of guilt and shame
- Under- or overachieving at school
- Hearing degrading language and threats
- Seeing property destruction
- Living with bruises and tears
- Fear of parents getting a divorce
- Fear of dad going to jail

[5] *Permission to use "My Daddy is a Monster" granted by National Coalition Against Domestic Violence, Denver, Colorado.*

4. Key Issues for Children

Summarize the above list by communicating the following key issues for children in violence. Write on the chalkboard:

Children feel:

Powerless....... because they can't stop the violence.

Confused....... because it doesn't make sense.

Angry .... because it shouldn't be happening.

Guilty .... because they think they've done something wrong.

Sad.............. because it's a loss.

Afraid .... because they may be hurt, they may lose someone they love, others may find out.

Alone .... because they think it's happening only to them.[6]

Ask the group to discuss their feelings related to what children feel.

5. Key Needs of Children

Talk about what children in abusive homes *need*. Include the following in the discussion:

- To be listened to and believed
- To have a safe place to express their feelings
- To be told that they are not alone
- To be told the violence is not their fault
- To have support from family, friends, counselors, or all of these
- To learn that conflict can be resolved without abuse
- To develop their own personal power

6. Participants' Feelings as Children

Finally, ask group members for their heartfelt thoughts about children. Ask them to think about when they were children and how the child within them felt about:

- How happiness was expressed in their family
- How sadness was expressed in their family
- How anger was expressed in their family
- How love or affection was expressed in their family

If there is time, pass out paper and crayons or markers to each group member. Ask group members to take a few minutes to draw a picture of a time or an event in their childhood involving their family. Suggest that they might want to

---

[6] *Adapted from* Children's Domestic Abuse Program, *developed by Wilder Foundation Community Assistance Program and published by Kidsrights, Charlotte, North Carolina.*

think about sounds, smells, and expressions related to their families. Ask group members to share their pictures and to comment on how they felt while drawing and how they think their children might be experiencing some of the same feelings. Encourage group members to imagine how the event they are drawing would have felt when they were children.

Break

7. Individual Time Taking

8. Closing

Suggest that one of the best things we can do for our children is to take care of ourselves. Ask group members to close with one way to take care of themselves this week.

Issues

1. *Some group members will not have any children.*
   Most groups will have a few women who have never had children or parented children. Ask group members without children to think about their own childhood as they participate in this session or about the children of friends or relatives who may be in abusive homes. If there are several group members without children, this session topic usually will not be selected.

2. *Some group members believe that their children have not been affected by the abuse.*
   If overt abuse has never occurred in the children's presence, it is easy for a group member to believe that the children are unaware of the abuse. Communicate that there is an underlying tension in abusive homes that few children will escape. Even if the child has not observed abuse directly, the child is aware of the covert abuse or the abuse that is more subtle and indirect. Counselors often hear from children that they know things their parents think are secrets. Also, adults frequently report that as children they were awakened in the night by the abuse and heard things that by day were not acknowledged in any way. This became part of the conspiracy of silence for them.

3. *Group members will state that they do not want their children to grow up being abused or abusive.*
   This is one of the most important hopes of abused women. They know the feelings of violation and wish that their children would never have the same experience. It is important to talk about how children learn from what they see and that, as parents, we are constantly modeling ways for our children to act. Growing up witnessing abuse does not mean children will grow up to be in abusive relationships, but they are at higher risk. Stress the points about what children in abusive homes need in order to address this issue.

4. *Group members will request resources for their children to address the abuse.*
   Facilitators should be aware of community resources for children. If domestic abuse groups for children exist in your area, talk about them. Many group members are unaware of groups for children. Ask the group members about resources they may have used. The group often has a wealth of information about resources. Suggest contacting school counselors for information.

5. *Some group members will want to discuss punishment or discipline of children in relation to acting-out behaviors.*
   Acknowledge that most children have some anger related to the abuse and that it can be difficult for parents to manage. Suggest that group members may want to get some parenting support but that, due to time constraints, addressing punishment and discipline in this group is not feasible. However, point out that you strongly advocate no hitting or spanking of children, as physical punishment tends to promote fear. Family Support Network (which has been called Parents Anonymous in the past) might be mentioned as one resource. You might also have some handouts or books you can offer that would be helpful for asking for more parenting information.

6. *The list of Key Issues for Children on page 105 can be used as a handout in group.*
   The feelings summarized in Key Issues for Children are significant information for mothers. This is a concise list of what children feel and experience, along with explanations about why they feel what they do. Such information may be extremely helpful for moms to better understand what their children are feeling.

7. *Drawing a picture of a childhood time or event with one's family can evoke different feelings for group members.*
   When art therapy is used to address family of origin memories, feelings often surface. Be prepared particularly for feelings of sadness as the pictures are shared. In the interest of available group time, suggest that the group support each other during the break. If this does not feel as if it would work, take extra time to work through any feelings that arise.

Notes, comments, and observations:

Cluster 3

Abuse-Related Issues
for Women

Assertiveness

Goals

In this session, participants will:

1. Understand what assertiveness means.
2. Understand the differences between assertive, passive, aggressive, and passive-aggressive behaviors.
3. Be aware of personal safety issues related to assertive behaviors.
4. Identify personal situations that cause difficulty in being assertive.
5. Develop an assertiveness plan that can be used for many situations.
6. Understand that there are benefits and potential negative consequences when establishing assertive behaviors.

Format

Women in our culture traditionally have *not* been taught that assertiveness is a good thing. Instead, they may have been encouraged to ignore what they want and need, or hope that someone else will guess what they want and need. This session will help women gain an understanding of assertiveness.

1. Check-In

2. Assertiveness Defined

Explain to the group that assertiveness is a new concept for some women. Explain that in our culture, assertiveness has usually gone without reward, particularly for women. Remind them that, as females, we are often trained and encouraged to nurture and please at the expense of ignoring our own needs. It is difficult to be assertive if we have had little modeling and minimal practice at it.

Tell the group that we are going to approach the topic of assertiveness by looking at the behaviors that are often more familiar to us (passive, aggressive, and passive-aggressive) than those which we use less (assertive behaviors). Write on the chalkboard: Passive, Aggressive, and Passive-aggressive.

Ask some of the following questions:

- Are these terms familiar?

- How might these terms relate to boundaries?

- Do people get their way with these behaviors? What do people gain or lose?

- How does it feel when your partner behaves in any of these ways?

Next, ask the group to help define these three terms with words, phrases, or examples from their own experience. Following are some of the responses you may hear; you may want to add any of the following to the group's list:

Passive	*Aggressive*	*Passive-Aggressive*
Giving in	Creates conflict	Mean-spirited
Quiet	Abusive	Intentionally forgetful
Doormat	Intimidating	Resents others
Few opinions	Blaming	Subtly negative
One's own needs are unimportant	Hostile	Faults others
Self-defeating	Forceful	Feels unjustly treated
Isolated	Inappropriate anger	Hostile dependency
Avoids conflict	Demanding	Lacks responsibility for own behaviors
Taken advantage of	Attacking	Wants needs "guessed" by others
Rights are relinquished	Getting your way	Hurts through silence
Wants are not okay	Derogatory name calling	Simmering volcano
Too agreeable	Sabotaging	Builds anger and resentment
Don't "rock the boat"	Sarcasm	Uncooperative
Other's needs come first	Frequent yelling	
	Threatening	

When the responses are completed for the three types of behavior listed, ask some of the following questions:

- How does this list make you feel?

- How does it fit with your experience?

- How does it relate to the behaviors of your abusive partner?

Now write the word "Assertive" on the chalkboard, and ask the group for their definition and thoughts on this behavior. Following are responses you may hear:

Assertive

Respectful messages	Accepts responsibility
Clear communication	Looks for win/win solutions
Desire to solve problems	Understands wants are okay, even if not met
Directness	Willing to state feelings
Uses "I" statements	Thinking about yourself
Saying "no" is acceptable	Good self-care
Appropriate	Confident

3. Assertiveness and Safety

Then ask some of the following questions:

- Are assertive behaviors ones that you have been taught or encouraged to have?
- Would you like to become more assertive?
- Is it safe to be assertive in your abusive relationship?
- How would others in your life act if you tried being assertive?

Take this opportunity to remind group members that being assertive in an abusive relationship has some risks and that each member is the only one who can judge what is safe for her related to being assertive. Stress the importance of safety.

Next, pass out the Assertiveness Situations worksheet in Appendix G, page 186. Take a few minutes to fill this out. Go around the group and ask members to share the situations they circled on the worksheet and any other personal difficulties they filled in on numbers 21 and 22. Now ask each group member to think about one assertiveness issue she would like to work on in the next week. Suggest that it might be safest for them to choose a situation that does not involve their abusive partner.

4. Assertiveness Plans

Now pass out the Assertiveness Exercise worksheet in Appendix G, page 187. Ask each member to identify her situation or problem, the person with whom she would like to speak about the problem, how she could formulate a plan to do that, and whether or not she needs to set a time to speak to the person.

Stress that assertiveness involves stating how you feel and what you want. Write on the chalkboard the following statement:

When I feel _____ because of _____ ,
I need to _____ and I want _____ .

Then write the following feeling words on the board and state that these words are often related to a lack of assertiveness. This list will be helpful for group members as they do the above exercise.

Typical feelings		
Used	Hurt	Intimidated
Selfish	Boastful	Afraid/Scared
Unworthy	Annoyed	Bothersome
Embarrassed		

Go around the group again, asking each group member to practice her personal situation using the "When I feel" statement on the chalkboard. She can use the feeling words listed on the board or any other feelings she may have. Give an example before the group begins, such as:

> When I feel *scared* . . .
> because of *your mood* . . .
> I need to *distance myself from you* . . .
> and I want *you to understand that I'm trying to prevent a conflict between us.*

Summarize this exercise with the following questions:

- How did it feel to practice being assertive?
- Do you want to follow through with your assertiveness plan this week?
- Are you fearful of repercussions from becoming assertive?
- Are you keeping your personal safety a top priority when using assertive behavior?

5. Benefits and Negative Consequences of Assertiveness

Briefly talk about the benefits of being assertive and the possible negative consequences from other people. You can expect to hear the following:

Benefits	*Negative Consequences*
Personal power	Upsetting the status quo
Internal well-being	Immature behaviors by others
Self-respect	Revengeful responses by others
Feelings of independence	Aggressive reactions by others
Improved boundaries	Blaming behaviors by others
Mature behavior	Inappropriate anger by others
Meeting one's own needs	Abuse of any kind

Last, go around the group and ask each member to comment on what was the most helpful part of this session for her. Ask group members to be prepared to check-in next week with the results of the assertiveness homework exercise.

Break

6. Individual Time Taking

7. Closing

Issues

1. *Assertiveness is often a new concept for group members.*
   Most group members have heard this term but do not really understand the actual concept and how it works. They may also be confused about related terms like passive, aggressive, and passive-aggressive. Spend time sorting out the differences between these terms so that group members can understand the importance of the concept of assertive behavior covered later in the session.

2. *Many group members have not had assertive behavior modeled for them.*
   In our culture, assertive behavior by women has typically been discouraged and criticized. Because of this, we often do not know how to be assertive and to get our needs known and met in an appropriate manner. It will be extremely important for you as the facilitator to model assertive behavior and to point out when group members are being assertive. Validating group members for taking risks related to assertive behavior may help give their peers the courage to take risks as well.

3. *Safety issues for group members related to assertive behaviors CANNOT BE OVERSTRESSED.*
   Group members who are living with their abusive partners or have to interact with abusive ex-partners cannot be warned too much about considering their safety and any possible negative consequences related to their assertive behavior. Only the individual member can decide what is best for her physical and emotional well-being when taking risks on assertive behavior. DO NOT under any circumstances encourage members to take any risks that are not comfortable and safe for them when trying out new assertive behaviors. The group member's safety is always the top priority when she is interacting with an abusive partner.

4. *Encourage group members to be creative with personal situations that pose difficulties related to assertiveness.*
   The situations listed in the Assertiveness Exercise are general and do not begin to cover the many situations women experience. Allow for a few extra minutes to think of the personal situations that should be addressed. Suggest that group members add these to the list.

5. *Stress the benefits of assertive behavior.*
   Talk about how being assertive is the middle ground or the balancing point between passive and aggressive. Assertiveness means getting what we want by asking for it. Passivity is expecting others to figure out what we want, and aggressiveness means just taking what we want. The latter behaviors fail over time, as there are inherent problems in both ways of behaving. The benefits of assertive behavior include gaining a sense of empowerment to care for yourself and the knowledge that asking for what you want is legitimate.

Notes, comments, and observations:

Boundaries

Goals

In this session, participants will:

1. Establish a group definition of boundaries.
2. Identify boundary issues related to family of origin and self-identity.
3. Understand the impact of blurred boundaries for abused women.
4. Explore the relationship between childhood boundary issues and adult boundary issues, and connect how these relate to abusive relationships.
5. Identify specific examples of boundary violations that are abusive.
6. Role play setting boundary limits.
7. Identify ways to begin building good boundaries.

Format

Boundaries are often violated in abusive relationships. When we live or interact with a person who violates our boundaries, we begin to lose sight of what appropriate boundaries are. This session will explore the concept of appropriate and good boundaries.

1. Check-In

2. Boundaries Defined

To prepare the group for this session, begin with a brief discussion on boundaries in general. You might present a brief overview that addresses some of these questions:

- Why do a session on boundaries?
- How do we, as women, learn about appropriate and inappropriate boundaries?

- Do good and bad boundaries vary from person to person, culture to culture?
- How can we know when someone is violating our boundaries?
- How do we know when we are violating another person's boundaries?
- What do you think about setting healthy boundaries and limits?

Now, as a group, we will try to define what a boundary is. Ask the group to offer their ideas. You may want to offer some of the following ideas as well.

> *What is a boundary?*
> - A concept that helps us to define ourselves and our identity.
> - A limit on how far we can go with comfort in a relationship.
> - A space that defines both the physical and psychological well-being between people.
> - A means to protect ourselves.
> - A filter to determine how we act or what we say.

3. Blurred Boundaries

Next, tell the group that in this session we will try to evaluate how our boundaries have been violated by our partners and others *and* how we have violated the boundaries of others, often unknowingly.

To look at the way negative or blurred boundaries begin, it is important to be aware that there are three parts to our self or identity:

- Intellectual self
- Emotional self
- Physical self

In these three areas, our boundaries can often become blurred, affecting what other people will do to us and what we might do to others as well. Usually, we learn blurred boundaries from our family of origin. Write on the chalkboard and ask for the group's ideas in each of the three areas. You may want to suggest any of the following examples in each category.

Boundary Blurring

Intellectual:
- Thoughts and ideas are discounted
- Unclear rules
- Mind-reading expectations
- Lack of choices
- Differences and individuality are discouraged

Physical:
- Sexual abuse
- Date rape
- Treated as an object
- Lack of privacy
- Lack of appropriate touching

Emotional:
- Feelings discounted
- Abandonment issues
- Family secrets
- Role problems
- Needs and wants not acknowledged

Given these examples of how we may have experienced blurred boundaries in our lives, how might this experience affect us as adults? In our abusive relationships? Ask group members to share their personal experiences and ideas about this. Things you might expect to hear or add include:

- Erosion of self-identity
- Unsure of self; low self-esteem
- Failure to assess danger accurately
- Blames self for anything and everything
- Isolates self; fails to reach out to others
- Lack of energy
- Abuse occurs
- Can't say "no" to requests
- Difficulty trusting others

4. Boundary Violations in Abusive Relationships

Next, directly connect the impact of blurred boundaries to being abused. Ask the following questions for discussion:

- What are the similarities of blurred boundaries in your family of origin and in your abusive relationship?
- What feelings did you have as a child that are similar to feelings you have experienced when you've been abused as an adult?
- What did you blame yourself for as a child that you also blame yourself for in your abusive relationship?
- How did/do either of your parents/caregivers remind you of your abusive partner?

Talk about how boundaries are violated or feel invaded in abusive relationships. Tell the group that they will look at boundary problems and talk about specific examples of violations in specific areas. Suggest that these areas have to do with respect for oneself and respect for other people. Explain that people often become confused about boundaries when they grow up with little information and no modeling of acceptable boundaries. As they reflect on personal boundary problems, they can begin to see how they might fail to protect themselves by not being able to set limits.

Write the following six terms on the board. Ask the group to give examples of boundary violations in each area. Point out that these areas can overlap. You could include any of the following examples:

Time:
- Expectation to drop what you're doing to meet another's demands
- Having a curfew as a grown woman
- Starting a fight as you are about to leave for work or other appointment

Space:
- Purses and drawers are not private space
- Accusations of what you've been doing when you are away
- Getting physically too close to you when in conflict

Property:
- Taking or using things without asking
- Destruction of personal property, meant to be personally hurtful
- Taking of car keys to prevent one from leaving

Privacy:
- Reading your mail or journal
- Listening in on phone conversations
- Demanding you account for all your time

Sexual:
- Lack of privacy in bathroom
- Making negative comments on your size and shape
- Saying no to sexual intercourse is not accepted

Feelings:
- Telling you what you "should" feel
- Being thought of as wrong, ridiculous, bad, overly sensitive, and so forth
- Being taunted, mimicked or belittled for having feelings

The ideal is being able to recognize violations and set limits on what one will or will not accept from another person's behavior. Of course, this is the ideal. An abused woman may not be able to safely set a boundary or limit on her abusive partner. Again, each member must decide what is best for her related to setting boundaries and her safety.

5. Practice Sessions: Setting Limits

Ask the group to choose one boundary violation from the chalkboard on which they would like to practice setting a limit during the next week, either with their partners or with another significant person in their lives. Ask that they identify the following:

- The area they want to work on
- The boundary violation
- The person with whom the limit will be set
- How this limit will be set

Suggest that writing in their journal about their feelings, their fears, and the results of setting limits would be helpful. Ask that they plan to check in about this assignment at the next session.

As a final step, ask for a volunteer who would like to practice setting a boundary or limit in the group as a role play with another group member. Have the volunteer identify the points above and ask the second person to become the person with whom the limit will be set. Often the second person will play the abusive partner. Ask the other group members observing to give support and encouragement for staying safe when setting limits with abusive partners.

6. Building Good Boundaries

Discuss as a group how people can begin to change their boundary behavior and begin to build good boundaries for themselves. Use the three identity areas of intellectual, emotional, and physical to do this exercise. Write on the chalkboard:

Building Good Boundaries

Intellectually:
- Okay to ask questions
- Can think and speak for self
- Alone time can be healthy
- Awareness of right to make mistakes

Emotionally:
- Can allow self a range of feelings
- Learns to trust another person
- Shares inner secrets with safe person
- States feelings when appropriate

Physically:
- Aware of own body needs and space
- Esteems one's own body
- Expression of sexuality as a choice rather than an obligation
- Rights to personal property

Summarize by saying that the results of good boundaries are:

- We know who we are
- We can express our feelings
- We can make choices
- We can be responsible
- We are true to our own values

Boundaries allow us to maintain the distinction between ourselves and others.

Break

7. Individual Time Taking

8. Closing

Issues

1. *Sometimes a member will not relate to experiencing blurred boundaries as a child.*
   Some group members will have had or will see their families as loving, nurturing, and having good boundary definition. When this is the case, a group member might be particularly confused about the abuse as an adult and how it happened to her. You can talk about boundary problems and abusive behavior by partners to some degree as an element of bad luck or unfortunate circumstances and not something that group members bring on themselves.

2. *Establishing good boundaries can be dangerous for some group members.*
   As you address abuse, it is absolutely necessary that you always remind group members that they are in the best position to decide what is safe for them. As facilitators, we cannot afford to make choices for group members about setting boundaries or in which areas they should try to set limits with their partners. Safety is always the first consideration.

3. *As a group facilitator, you are in an excellent position to model good boundaries.*
   Your behavior is constantly watched by the group members—even your most seemingly inconsequential actions. This gives you a lot of responsibility to know and understand your own boundaries and how you set limits around them. A good example of this might be a group member asking a personal question that feels inappropriate to you. The way you handle this situation models for the group what your boundaries are and how you respond to a boundary violation.

4. *Be prepared to give examples of boundary violations as you proceed with this session.*
   Real-life examples of boundary violations against women are helpful in clarifying what is a negative or blurred boundary. Use examples from your own life or examples from past groups (be mindful of protecting participant confidentiality when using stories of past participants). Each boundary violation will eventually remind you of a story or incident tucked away somewhere in your memory.

5. *Personal disclosures about boundary issues can be helpful to the group.*
   Discussing your own boundary issues can be very appropriate as long as you understand the difference between disclosure for the benefit of the group versus disclosure that helps you do personal work on your own boundary issues. This is always a fine line, but appropriate and timely self-disclosure can be a powerful teaching tool.

6. *Role-playing is difficult for many group members.*
   When you ask group members to volunteer to role play setting limits, some members may be too nervous or frightened. If no volunteers come forward, demonstrate by yourself, showing a common boundary issue like saying no to a request. Then ask again if someone would like to give role-playing a try. Usually with a little encouragement on your part, someone will volunteer.

You can also ask the group members to help each other with the role-plays. For example, have one member sit next to and coach the woman who is role-playing her situation. The "coach" can give her some words or ideas that may be helpful in stimulating role play responses.

Notes, comments, and observations:

Women and Sexuality

Goals

In this session, participants will:

1. Identify confusion related to their sexuality.
2. Explore the unhealthy and healthy aspects of sexual relationships.
3. Describe insights and feelings related to sexuality.
4. Identify ways that self-esteem related to a woman's sexuality can be supported and enhanced.
5. Develop a personalized plan working towards healthy sexuality and self-esteem.

Format

The joy of being a sexual woman is often damaged in an abusive relationship. Intimacy is lost and confusion sets in. Women are entitled to feel sexually healthy and to know what that might be like in a caring relationship.

1. Check-In

2. Confusion about Sexuality

Introduce this session by talking about how women historically have not felt comfortable or free to discuss their sexuality or sexual feelings. Group members are frequently unaware of how sexuality is related to loving themselves and others. In this culture, sex is often used to advertise material goods and can be an issue of dominance. Thus, it is often difficult for group members to look at their sexuality as a positive, safe, and joyful part of their lives.

Women who are in abusive relationships often feel confused about their sexuality. Hurtful behaviors by partners range from total sexual withdrawal to sexual assault and physical harm. Sexual *intimacy* does not exist in the relationship, and women are often left feeling empty and ashamed. Begin an open discussion on women and sexuality by asking some of the following questions:

- What is confusing about a woman's sexuality?
- How do our partner's behaviors contribute to not feeling good about our sexuality?
- Is there conflict about sexual values between you and your partner?
- Do you feel exploited sexually?

3. Healthy Aspects of Sexual Relationships

After a short discussion has begun to open up the thought process around a woman's sexuality, tell the group that they are going to look at individual sexuality by drawing two aspects of it. Provide large paper and crayons or markers and ask that each member divide her picture into two parts. On one side of the paper, ask group members to draw the sexual part of them that has felt exploited, hurt, ashamed, nonconsensual, or maltreated. On the other half of the paper, draw how a healthy, consensual, intimate, and pleasurable sexual self might look. Write these words describing healthy and unhealthy sexuality on the chalkboard for reference. Suggest that group members take a few moments to think about this and how it could be represented in a drawing. Allow ten to fifteen minutes to complete this. Encourage the group members to find a quiet place to do their drawing.

When the pictures are completed, return to the circle and ask the group how it felt to consider their sexuality by expressing it through drawing. Was it a positive experience to think about this aspect of themselves? Did it bring up positive or negative feelings?

Now ask each group member to share her picture with the group, tell a little about the picture, and talk about what she might have learned about herself and her feelings related to her sexuality. Suggest that the group can make observations and offer support and validation for any feelings that arise. Allow sufficient time to discuss the pictures.

4. Supporting Self-Esteem

Summarize this session by talking about how women can support one another about their sexuality and begin to build on their self-esteem related to it. Ask for the group's ideas and offer some of the following. Write on the chalkboard:

Support and Esteem for Women's Sexuality

- Sexuality is expressed from birth to death.
- Our culture associates sex with shame.
- Sexual feelings and fantasies are normal and natural.
- Women are entitled to equal power in their sexual relationships.
- Talking and communicating freely with each other about our sexuality is positive.
- Feeling safe is crucial to being vulnerable in our sexual partnerships.
- As women grow and change, their sexuality may also change.

- Sexuality can be quiet and dormant at times and noisy and active at other times.
- Women are sexual beings alone as well as with partners.
- Women have the right to choices when being sexual—when, how, and with whom.
- Exploring myths about women and sexuality is important to understanding ourselves.
- Manipulation by a partner to be sexually active is a misuse of power. Women have the right not to be obligated to be sexual.

Ask each group member to choose two areas from this list that she would like to work on related to enhancing her self-esteem associated with sexuality. Go around the circle and have each member share her two choices. Ask for a plan on how this process will be carried out.

Break

5. Individual Time Taking

6. Closing

Issues

1. *Women and sexuality is a broad topic.*
   Many approaches can be taken to explore women and sexuality. This session is only one way to relate a group member's abuse to her sexuality. Facilitators should feel free to develop and create sessions that explore a woman's sexuality using other approaches.

2. *The art therapy exercise may cause many different emotions to surface.*
   When group members are asked to draw an abusive experience in any way, there is always a potential for feelings to erupt that are difficult and sometimes unexpected. Be prepared to process feelings and work through flashbacks if necessary. Look to the group to give support and encouragement to each other.

3. *Group members will share sexual abuse stories that are shocking.*
   Be prepared as a facilitator to avoid being shocked by any type of sexual abuse. Nevertheless, group members might still communicate their shock. It becomes your job to normalize these reactions and assure women sharing their story that there is nothing wrong with them and that they are not to blame for a partner's sexually abusive behavior towards them.

4. *Group members will feel shame about their sexuality and sexual abuse.*
   Be observant of group members who feel ashamed. Look for lack of eye contact or for eyes dropping to the floor. Gently ask how a member feels about what she has shared. Ask the group for their feedback and support to help her move beyond the feelings of shame.

5. *Group members may be uneducated about their bodies in relation to their sexuality.*
   Suggest that group members do some self-education and self-exploration of their bodies to build their esteem. There are many good books about women's sexuality. Stress the importance of knowing one's own self sexually and how women's bodies work, as well as the need to become sexually empowered as women.

Notes, comments, and observations:

Questions about Men Who Batter

Goals

In this activity, participants will:

1. Ask questions of a male counselor who has worked with men who batter.

2. Have an opportunity to hear what occurs in a men's domestic abuse group from a male counselor's perspective.

3. Receive information about what can and cannot be accomplished in addressing men's violence in treatment.

4. Be able to engage in a safe, supportive, and honest dialogue with a male counselor in an attempt to address questions and concerns about being victims of male violence.

5. At the end of the session, process the feelings and thoughts of the group related to the information that was presented.

Format

This optional session is frequently chosen (see page 7). Timing is important. It is best to offer the session near the end of the program, around the thirteenth or fourteenth session.

At the end of the preceding session, ask the group members to think about their questions and issues related to batterers' behaviors, treatment, and other related issues. *Always* offer the option to not attend or not participate in this session. Almost without exception, all members of the group will attend and participate at whatever level they feel comfortable.

1. Check-In

2. Questions for the Male Counselor

The women's group counselor and the male guest presenter agree ahead of time about whether they go into the group together or if the women's counselor wants to do a quick check-in *before* the presenter comes into the group room. Most of the time, they choose to go in together and do a brief introduction of the guest and a brief check-in with the presenter in the group.

After the check-in, the women's group facilitator again reviews with the group what the session is about. Basically, state that the next hour or so will be open to asking questions of the male presenter about men's domestic abuse treatment and other issues related to men's abuse against women.

Typically the male counselor says a few things about his experience in working with men who batter. The presenter may also want to establish some general or specific guidelines such as letting the group know that any question is all right to ask. However, the presenter also has permission to decline to respond or answer questions that are too personal or reveal confidential information about participants.

For example, if one of the group members asked about her partner's progress in group because she knows that the presenter is her partner's counselor, the presenter could not reveal any of this information. In fact, the presenter could not acknowledge in any way that he even knows her partner. The laws of confidentiality must be followed. The women's group counselor can prepare the group the week before to prevent these situations from occurring.

Responses to personal questions like "Have you ever been abusive?" are up to the presenter; he must determine his own comfort level with these types of questions. Appropriate and clear boundaries should be practiced.

After introductions, the presenter opens up the session to the group members to begin to ask questions. Typically the questions lead to a very open and free-flowing dialogue. Time often passes quickly. Generally, if the session is going well, the one-hour time frame is extended another twenty to thirty minutes. End the session with enough time for a break and time to discuss the experience after the presenter leaves.

The following questions are often asked by group members:

- Does the men's program cover the same information as the women's program?
- Do the men see themselves as being abusive?
- Why are men abusive?
- How can you tell if a man is abusive before dating or marrying him?
- What is the success rate in the men's program?
- Do you think that once a man is abusive he will always be abusive?
- If a man doesn't want to change, can anything help?
- Do the men really see how much hurt and pain they put their partners and children through?
- If he has a drinking/drug problem, will domestic abuse counseling help?
- How many men do you think will never be abusive after treatment?

- How do I get my partner to go into treatment?

- Do you think their abuse problem is hereditary?

- I see my teenage son starting to act just like his father, and it scares me to death. What should I do?

- I have constantly met roadblock after roadblock with the system. It seems that the system refuses to take my concerns seriously. What do you recommend?

- I want to stay with my partner, but he won't go to a domestic abuse group. He said he will go to couples or marital counseling. What do you think about couples counseling?

- He tells me that the abuse is my fault or that I'm equally responsible for the abuse. How do you deal with the men in group on this issue?

- My husband is in a domestic abuse group, and it sounds like it's a "good old boys" club. I don't think he's learned a thing—in fact, he's gotten worse. What do you think? Is he learning how to be a better abuser from his group?

- Did most abusers grow up in abusive homes and that's why they're abusive?

- My partner says he'll kill me if I leave him. Do you think I should believe him?

- Do the men ever talk about their sexual abuse against women?

- How do you find "good" men who won't abuse you? It seems like all men are jerks.

- How can I trust the counselor in the men's group that my partner is in? I've tried to contact him regarding my partner, but he says the information is confidential.

- Do you think that men who batter should be locked up?

- My partner is from a minority culture and says he doesn't want some white counselor telling him what to do. What do you say to that?

- Are you married? Have you ever been abusive?

- Would you recommend that I get a divorce and get out while I still can?

- My partner thinks that I'm being brainwashed by a group of feminists and male bashers. How should I respond to him?

- Do the men really understand their role in the abuse?

This is a sample list of spontaneous questions that may be asked by group members. In addition to these types of questions, other issues may come up. The male presenter should discuss responses to them ahead of time with the women's facilitator. Here are some examples of issues that may arise:

- A group member has not acknowledged that any physical abuse has occurred in her relationship. She has been comparing her situation with those of the other women in the group. She questions to what extent she has been abused, yet she has talked about emotional and verbal abuse during the group. It is important that the male presenter address the seriousness of *all* types of abuse (not just physical).

- One or two group members dominate the questions and draw focus specifically to their own personal situations. If this situation arises, it's probably best if the group facilitator takes responsibility for directing the group or for individual group dynamics, since she has the relationship with the group members.

The women's facilitator should also feel free to ask questions as she sees necessary to cover areas that have been missed. It's best, too, if the women's facilitator sets the time limit and ends the question and answer session when she sees fit. Allow time to process the experience after the male presenter leaves.

After this session, some of the group members may experience a loss of hope or come to an emotional realization of something they may have feared all along—*treatment for men who batter may not produce the results they anticipated.* Help women understand that there is no magic to treatment for men who have abused their partners. This is no easy task. Most men who enter domestic abuse treatment programs have no idea what is in store for them. In fact, many come involuntarily and have not even acknowledged a need to change.

Because the presenter has provided a realistic account of the complexity that exists in abusive relationships, group members may experience highly intense feelings, ranging from hopelessness to a sense of resolve. Give each member an opportunity to express her feelings and thoughts in the group prior to ending the session. You may even need to revisit the topic in the next week's session.

Break

3. Individual Time Taking

4. Closing

Issues

1. *It is important to consider the risk of doing this session.*
   This is a risky session to present, but it has the potential to be a very beneficial session. However, if it is not presented in a sensitive, timely, and appropriate manner, this session can have some serious short-term results such as poor role-modeling, placing blame back on a woman, or contradicting the program philosophy.

2. *The male presenter for this session must be sensitive to women's issues.*
   The most critical factor in determining if this session should be offered to the group is that the male presenter is aware of and sensitive to the issues that women who have been battered face. This means many things, but most importantly it means that the female facilitator determines the male presenter's level of competence regarding this crucial issue.

   We recommend that the group facilitator meet with the potential male presenter and go through a list of questions like those previously given. The facilitator should be aware of the male presenter's knowledge about perpetrators and victims of abuse, assess the presenter's boundaries and insights, and determine if their program philosophies and principles are similar.

Consider your intuitive sense that the presenter can be trusted with the emotional well-being of the group. If you have any concerns, these should be addressed. *Always* err on the side of caution. If there are any doubts about the male presenter's ability to address the women's group, it would be better *not* to offer this session than to potentially put the group members at an emotional risk. (Note: If there is a male cofacilitator in your group who has experience working with men who batter, he may be able to lead this session.)

3. *Ex-perpetrators may or may not be sensitive presenters in a women's group.* Finally, there may be the question of having an ex-perpetrator of domestic abuse present to the women's group. We have experimented with this situation in several of our programs (men's, women's, and adolescent). There is no correct answer to this question. Our experience tells us the potential exists for successful learning and dialogue to occur.

However, it is *extremely* risky to have a male perpetrator come to present in a women's group. Only under the best circumstances, taking many factors into account, would we suggest that any ex-perpetrator present in a woman's group. There are just too many things that could make this experience negative and potentially disturbing and damaging for all involved.

Notes, comments, and observations:

Cluster 4

Common Responses to Abuse Experiences

Shame and Guilt

Goals

In this session, participants will:

1. Understand the difference between shame and guilt.

2. Understand how the cycle of shame works.

3. Become aware of how to intervene in the cycle of shame.

4. Have ideas on how to move through shame to taking personal responsibility.

5. Understand the characteristics of a shame-based family.

Format

This session is often very helpful for women as they learn to understand how shame works in an abusive relationship. Their partner blames them for the abuse, and they blame themselves for the abuse. The vicious cycle of shame has begun. This session will examine that cycle in detail.

1. Check-In

2. Defining Shame and Guilt[7]

Introduce this session by writing the following on the chalkboard:

Shame	Guilt
I am a mistake.	I made a mistake.
I am a failure.	I failed to do something.
I am wrong.	My behavior is wrong.

---

[7] *The definition of shame and descriptions of shame and guilt used in this section ("2. Defining Shame and Guilt") were developed by Mary Jo Nissen, MA, LP, LICSW, St. Paul, Minnesota. Used by permission.*

Discuss with the group what they see as the difference between shame and guilt statements on the board. Help them understand the following definition:

Unhealthy shame is the faulty conviction that one is somehow innately defective, as compared to the norm.

Then talk about shame and guilt and how they differ. Share with the group the following characteristics of a person with a shame-based identity:

- Their sense of shame blocks learning
- They perceive themselves through a screen of shame
- They believe that amends cannot be made
- They believe they can never be forgiven
- They believe the negative experience of shame cannot be stopped
- Their shame is kept in secret

Characteristics of guilt:

- Guilt is specific (shame is generalized)
- Amends can be made to alleviate guilt
- Forgiveness can be received to alleviate guilt
- Guilt is a learning tool

Talk about shame related to families and communicate the following:

> ***Foundations of a shame-based family:***
> - Inappropriate and changing rules
> - Faulty communication patterns
> - Lack of boundaries
> - Role reversal (children forced into parenting or care taking roles)

In a shame-based family, it's not okay to think, feel, or notice things. Universal words like "all," "none," and "every" are often used. It's a world of right and wrong, all or nothing. The children often parent their own parents. Shame-based families can have any of the following issues or problems:

- Alcoholism
- Eating disorders
- Abandonment
- Silent treatment
- Physical abuse
- Emotional abuse
- Sexual abuse
- Gambling

3. The Cycle of Shame[8]

Shame is learned and is passed down to future generations.

Communicate to the group that shame goes to the core of a person's being and becomes part of their identity. Guilt involves how our conscience monitors our behavior, which helps us to see when we need to take responsibility for something.

The impact of shame is devastating for many people and is highly related to lack of self-esteem and to self-worth problems. Shame is a negative that is difficult to undo.

Guilt is far easier to cope with and understand. Guilt can actually be positive in that it works to our benefit in helping change our behavior.

Draw on the chalkboard:

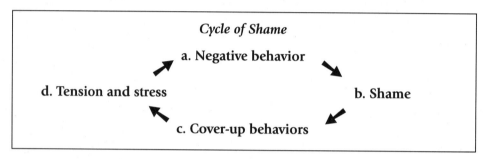

Cycle of Shame

a. **Negative behavior**

d. **Tension and stress**   b. **Shame**

c. **Cover-up behaviors**

Tell the group that you are going to give an example of how this works first. Ask them to think about an example they might share with the group as you fill in this cycle with an example of a woman who is overweight and has some compulsive eating habits.

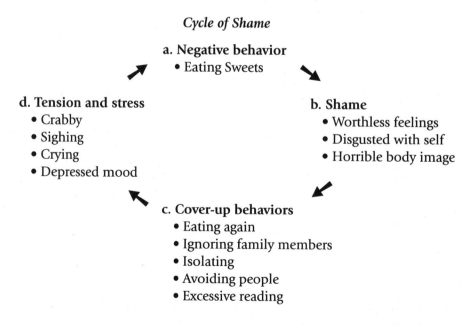

Cycle of Shame

a. **Negative behavior**
- Eating Sweets

b. **Shame**
- Worthless feelings
- Disgusted with self
- Horrible body image

c. **Cover-up behaviors**
- Eating again
- Ignoring family members
- Isolating
- Avoiding people
- Excessive reading

d. **Tension and stress**
- Crabby
- Sighing
- Crying
- Depressed mood

---

[8] *"Cycle of Shame" source unknown.*

4. Stopping the Cycle of Shame

Next, demonstrate how the shame cycle can be intervened upon anywhere in the process. It might look like this:

a. Negative behavior
- Notes to self on refrigerator
- No sweets in the house
- Behavior modification chart

d. Tension and stress
- Breathe deeply
- Positive self-talk
- Rent a funny video
- Take a warm bubble bath

b. Shame
- Tell someone what you have done
- Use affirmations
- Forgive yourself for not being perfect
- Find one part of your body that you like

c. Cover-up behaviors
- Interact with other people
- Find a support group
- Take a walk
- Call a supportive person

Ask for a group member's example for the shame cycle. Fill it out on the chalkboard, enlisting the entire group's help as the process takes place. Group members can help the woman identify the shame she feels, the cover-up behaviors, and how the tension and stress manifests itself. Next, go through the process of intervening in the shame cycle in all the areas.

Discuss how the shame cycle relates to abuse. Suggest that being abused can produce shame. This may result from believing that we are to blame or are at fault for another person's behavior, because somehow we provoked or caused the abuse.

5. Taking Responsibility

Talk about the ways women can move through shame to taking responsibility—not taking responsibility for another person's behavior, but taking responsibility for their own well-being. This is not an easy task and will take time but is well worth the effort. Ask for the group's ideas and participation in (write on chalkboard):

Ways to Move through Shame to Responsibility

- Translate the shame into pain. Talk about the pain in a safe and supportive environment.
- Aim for equal power in relationships. Respect your own and others' boundaries.
- Stop comparing yourself to others. Value yourself for who you are.
- Replace negative self-talk with affirmations.

- Be responsible for your behavior *only*.
- Build a supportive network.
- Move from shame to guilt. Give yourself permission to make mistakes and fail.
- Explore and work through the shame that you learned in your family.
- Allow and express your feelings.

Share this list of ideas with the group while adding their ideas. Be sure someone in the group records this list and hands it out the following week. Ask the group members to select one of these ways to move through shame and work on it in the next week, and share results during check-in at the following group session.

Break

6. Individual Time Taking

7. Closing

Issues

1. *The differences between shame and guilt can be confusing for some group members.*
   The meaning of shame and guilt and how they occur in our lives is a new concept for many women. Group members usually think of guilt and shame as the same thing. Members will work through this topic at different rates.

2. *Learning about shame is heartening for group members.*
   Seeing the cycle with real-life problems and ways to intervene in the problems gives women hope. They like understanding how this cycle works and appear to get comfort from understanding that there is a pattern with which they can identify.

3. *Abuse and shame are related.*
   Being abused contributes to a woman's shame. This is an important concept to address. Some group members believe they are at fault or to blame for the abuse done to them. This produces shame because they believe they could stop the abuse if they weren't such a failure. Other group members state that they know they are not responsible for the abuse. At some level, though, they take responsibility for their partner's abusive behavior without even being aware of it. As facilitators, we must listen for these subtle revelations and help women move through shame.

Notes, comments, and observations:

Grief and Loss

Goals

In this session, participants will:

1. Identify the meaning of grief and loss.

2. Identify losses in an abusive relationship.

3. Become aware of the significance of losing dreams.

4. Understand the grief process and how women respond to it.

5. Make a connection between grief, loss, and abuse.

6. Identify ways to care for themselves when experiencing grief.

Format

Most women do not think about abuse in terms of grief and loss. The reality, though, is that significant losses occur. A major one is loss of the dream of a loving and caring relationship. Recognizing that grief and loss exist is helpful for many women who are being abused.

1. Check-In

2. Defining Grief and Loss

Grief and loss have been widely researched and written about. They are common experiences for most of us. Grief is generally a healthy process related to dealing with loss. It is not usually something anyone chooses to do, but is often inevitable because of losses beyond their control and feelings they have about those losses. When one experiences loss, their lives become altered and are never quite the same again. They have the job of figuring out who they are and identifying themselves once again. This is the task of grief.

Ask the group if they can relate to being different after a loss of some kind. Next, tell the group that they are going to identify some of their losses, especially those related to abusive relationships. You might expect to hear some of the following (write on the chalkboard):

Losses in Abusive Relationships

- Self-esteem
- Marriage
- Friends/family
- Money/home
- Mental health
- Dreams of a happy relation-ship/family
- Innocence

- Sexual partner
- Desire for future relationships
- Physical health
- Security
- Future-oriented dreams
- Children's innocence and happiness

Briefly discuss the loss of hopes and dreams. Ask the group any of the following questions.

- Where did your dreams come from?

- What have your dreams looked like in your adult relationships?

- Are your dreams realistic?

- Which would you miss more: your abusive partner, or the dream of what you thought the relationship would be like?

- Does the dream keep you connected to a relationship that no longer feels right?

Suggest that many losses are related to the hopes and dreams of what group members wanted in life and in partner relationships. Many group members relate to this and become aware of why it feels so confusing and frightening to lose a person who is bringing them so much pain and unhappiness. Clarify the difference between the loss of a person and the loss of a dream to help members with confusion related to abuse.

Next, initiate a discussion on the process of grief. Restate for the group that the task of grief is to identify themselves again after a loss has occurred. Since life will never look quite the same again, they have to figure out who they are after the loss. Introduce the idea that grief is often thought of in stages and that many feelings arise when a person is grieving for a loss. People will often experience anger, denial, blame, guilt, and depression before arriving at acceptance of a loss. There is no particular order to these feelings, and a person can cycle in and out of them quite often. For example, one day is a good day and we feel acceptance around a loss, only to find ourselves sliding back into depression over the loss the following day. This is a normal grief process and is to be expected.

Now, ask the group some of the following questions about grief:

- Is grief automatic? Does everyone grieve or mourn over their losses?

- What might unresolved or "frozen" grief look like?

- What does it mean to see yourself differently after a loss?

- Do you need to allow time in your busy life to grieve?

- Does the passage of time take care of your grief?

- How do reactions from your family and friends affect your grief process?
- Is grieving for the loss of a partner, relationship, or marriage more difficult than other losses, such as a death?

3. Reactions to Grief and Loss

Many times people are in the midst of grieving and do not even recognize what is happening. Listing some of the reactions or symptoms related to grief and loss will help the group understand the grief process. Ask the group for their ideas on what occurs when they experience grief and loss. Write their ideas on the chalkboard. Expect to hear some of the following:

Responses to Grief and Loss

- Anger
- Impatience
- Over- or under-eating
- Sleep disturbance
- Depression
- Confusion
- Isolation

- Concentration problems
- Decision-making problems
- Blaming God, oneself, others
- Anxiety
- Emotional release
- Drug and alcohol abuse
- Inability to follow daily routine

---

4. Loss in Abusive Relationships

Ask the group if this list reminds them of anything else they have experienced. Does the list look similar to responses or reactions they have had to abuse? Suggest that the responses to grief and loss are closely related to their responses to abusive relationships. Connect the grief and loss to their abusive relationships.

5. Self-Care

Talk about what can be done to take care of themselves when experiencing grief. Write on the chalkboard:

Self-Care When in Grief

- Write in a journal
- Attend a support group
- Cry
- Exercise
- Seek individual therapy
- Talk to friends

- Understand the grief process
- Find time alone to reflect
- Reduce stress
- Keep change to a minimum
- Create a nurturing atmosphere
- Identify a support system

Ask each person to identify what she has done or would like to do from this list for her self-care plan.

Finally, ask the group members to discuss what it is like to develop a new sense of identity (to "re-identify" the self) after a significant loss. A good example of this is making behavioral and lifestyle changes after a relationship ends. You might ask some of the following questions:

- What new roles must you accept?
- How do your friendships change?
- How do your finances change?
- Do you have to relocate?
- Is depression a part of your experience?
- How does your family respond?
- Can it be positive to experience this loss?

Summarize this session by acknowledging how difficult the adjustment to a loss can be for group members. Encourage awareness and self-care when in grief.

Break

6. Individual Time Taking

7. Closing

Issues

1. *Grief and loss are typically thought of in terms of death and dying in our culture.*
   Women in abusive relationships have many kinds of losses in their lives. The focus for them is usually the loss of a partner and relationship due to some type of separation or divorce, rather than a death. The problem for women experiencing losses that are not related to death is that losses due to divorce or separation usually do not inspire the rallying of support and compassion that the loss through death does. Women are often left to their own devices when trying to acknowledge and work through losses that are typical to an abusive relationship. A woman may even be condemned or blamed for the loss of an abusive relationship by family, friends, children, and herself.

2. *It is helpful for group members to think of grief as a process of re-identifying the self after a loss occurs.*
   Grief involves looking for acceptance and new ways to function after a loss. Talking about how they see themselves and the new roles they have can be enlightening and sometimes even exciting for women. For example, when a loss is due to the breakdown of communication and intimacy in a relationship, a group member could decide how to function within that context. She can identify how she will operate differently as she learns to meet her own needs while still residing with her partner. This can be empowering for a group member as she begins to identify new ways to manage her life.

3. *Grieving is not a linear process.*
   Group members may go through many feelings and stages in the grieving process. It is important to know that a person can bounce around in the

different stages and feelings, have periods of acceptance, and then fall back into anger with a simple reminder of something related to the loss. Sometimes holidays and other significant dates, such as a wedding anniversary, will cause renewed grief.

4. ***Strength and courage, rather than time, heals all wounds.***
   There are many myths in our culture related to grief. "Time heals all wounds" fails to give credit to the person doing the grief work. It is important that group members pat themselves on the back for the many adjustments they make in the midst of many losses. Women are often taking on new roles and new responsibilities to survive losses involved in abusive relationships. Strength and courage, rather than time, may be the true healing factors. Validate the group members for their work so their healing process can continue.

5. ***Grief and loss is often a new concept in relation to abusive relationships.***
   Any time abuse occurs, whether we blame ourselves for it or not, a grieving process takes place. When we are being violated, there is a loss related to our human rights that causes us grief. Some women will openly acknowledge their grief and sadness and can hardly talk about it without crying. Other women will experience more of a "frozen grief" and are unaware of their internal process. As you talk about the concept of grief and loss related to abuse, new insights will develop for women, whether they are open or closed to their grieving process.

6. ***Some women will cry through the entire length of the group process.***
   As a facilitator, you need to know that some women enter the group in an extreme state of grief and may stay in that process for the entire sixteen weeks. This does not happen often, but it can occur. A woman in an emotional state of extreme grief may find it particularly difficult to talk in the group or to have any attention drawn to her. Be prepared to give a woman in such extreme grief plenty of space to be able to participate when she is ready to do so.

7. ***Shame occurs for some women who continue to want to be in a relationship that is causing them pain and grief.***
   This is a common experience for women in the group. It is helpful for women to become aware that they are not alone with their shame and confusion. Address this particular problem by talking about the difference between grief caused by the potential loss of a dream and grief caused by the loss of an abusive partner. Most women can see that the loss of the dream is what's holding them back, rather than the need for the abusive partner. Recognizing this can help to reduce the feelings of shame.

Notes, comments, and observations:

Depression

Goals

In this session, participants will:

1. Learn a general definition of depression.

2. Recognize symptoms of depression.

3. Explore possible causes of depression.

4. Identify the connection between depression and abuse.

5. Identify coping skills for dealing with a depressed mood.

6. Explore how depression might be seen as a gift.

Format

Depression is not unusual for women who are being abused. It may be that depression and oppression are related and that abused women suffer from depression when they are unsafe and unable to control their own lives. Learning more about depression often helps group members better understand themselves.

1. Check-In

2. Depression Defined

Begin this session by asking how many group members think they have experienced depression at one time or another in their lives. Ask how many felt embarrassed or ashamed about their depression and tried to keep others from knowing about it. Now briefly point out some general information that might be helpful in understanding depression and might help group members to understand that they are not alone with their depression.

- Women in abusive relationships often experience depression

- Depression appears to occur two times more frequently in women than in men

- Depression is characterized by an ongoing sense of hopelessness

- Depression is a widespread problem that can be treated
- Depression can be seen as a gift

Tell the group that there are many ways to define depression, but that for the purposes of this group, we will use the following definition. Write on the chalkboard:

Depression: a feeling or mood, accompanied by changes in behavior and thoughts, that affects the whole person—the body, mind, and spirit. It can lead to:

- Feelings of sadness and loneliness
- Withdrawal from people and activities
- Physical discomfort
- Loss of pleasure

Ask the group for their reaction to the definition. Can they relate to it? Allow time for a brief discussion of what has been presented so far.

Tell the group that symptoms of depression include:

1. Physical problems.
2. Changes in behavior.
3. Different feelings and thoughts.

Communicate that these three areas overlap. Ask the group to define symptoms in each category. The following are symptoms the group might mention:

Physical Problems	*Behavioral Changes*	*Thoughts and Feelings*
Chronic fatigue	Appetite changes	Indecisiveness
Lack of energy	Irritability	Emotional emptiness
Sleeping disturbances	Neglect of appearance	Feelings of hopelessness
Unexplained headaches	Concentration problems	Feeling highly self-critical
Digestive problems	Loss of sexual desire	Feeling overwhelmed

3. Causes of Depression

Next, discuss possible causes of depression. You can ask some of the following questions:

- Does abuse cause depression?
- Is there a relationship between anger and depression?
- What kinds of losses might contribute to depression?
- Does chemical imbalance play a role?
- Can depression be inherited/genetic?
- What about a person's environment? Neglect as a child? Relationship conflicts?
- How might a person's personality type contribute to depression? Passive? Dependent? Self-critical?

After having this discussion, point out that several factors may contribute to depression for any one person. Understanding the causes may not be as important as recognizing the symptoms so that the depression is not ignored or left untreated. Communicate that there is a difference between feeling blue or down now and then versus prolonged depressed feelings.

4. Link Between Abuse and Depression

Next, discuss the connection between abuse and depression. Ask the following questions:

- What does it feel like when someone systematically and repeatedly tries to have power and control over what you think and do?
- What does it feel like when you are isolated or kept away from contact with family and friends?
- How do feelings of craziness, confusion, and anger relate to depression?
- What is it like to usually or always put other people's needs ahead of your own needs?

After these four questions have been discussed, make the connection between abuse and depression. Help the group members see how feeling depressed is a normal response to not being or feeling in control or in charge of one's life. Communicate that there seems to be a significant correlation between abuse and depression and that many women who are being abused experience depression. Powerlessness is an extremely devastating feeling. All women who are abused feel powerless some of the time. It is difficult to overcome depression on your own when you feel powerless.

5. Coping with Depression

Next, pass out a sheet of paper (or have the group members write one out) that looks like this:

Things I Like to Do

When I am alone	When I am with someone else
1.	1.
2.	2.
3.	3.
4.	4.
5.	5.

Ask group members to spend a few minutes filling this out, and then ask each member to share her list. Ask them to circle their top choice in each category. Have group members share favorite things to do from their lists. Suggest that they can add new ideas that they hear from other group members. Suggest that when a person feels depressed, it is often difficult to think of what action they can take that will help. Suggest keeping this list somewhere close by to use when they feel depressed. If they can't contact another person, they can do one of the things from their "alone" list.

Next, suggest that there are ways to view depression as a gift or as a positive in their lives. This is usually a foreign concept and will need some discussion. Write on the chalkboard:

Depression as a Gift[9]

- Increased attention to spiritual life
- More empathy towards others
- Greater depth of emotional experience

- Opportunity for truths to emerge
- Awareness of pressures on oneself
- Greater acceptance of oneself

Ask for the group's response to these ideas.

Finally, discuss ideas or actions one might take to cope with depression. These actions might include individual therapy, seeing a physician, evaluation for medication, an exercise program, changes in dietary or alcohol consumption, avoiding extra stress, lowering expectations of oneself, and taking breaks to do something pleasurable.

Break

6. Individual Time Taking

7. Closing

Issues

1. *Depression varies in type and severity.*
   Three common types of depression exist: major depression, dysthymia, and manic-depression. Depression and its symptoms vary in severity and affect individuals differently. Symptoms may range from a mild impact on activities to complete immobilization and withdrawal.

2. *Suicide ideation and/or suicide attempts may be an issue when discussing depression.*
   Many group members will reveal their thoughts about suicide or past attempts at suicide during this session. It is not uncommon for at least a few group members to disclose this; help them process this to reduce the shame surrounding past suicide attempts. It is important to be prepared to ask questions and intervene if any group member states she is suicidal at this time.

3. *Antidepressant medication and its impact and side effects may become a topic for discussion during this session.*
   Some group members have fears about medications and what they might do to a person. Some believe medications are addictive and that people are often overmedicated. Be prepared to explain that we are all "wired" differently, that

---

[9] *"Depression As a Gift" from a presentation on Friday, October 7, 1994 at The College of St. Catherine by Kathy Cronkite, author of* On the Edge of Darkness: Conversations about Conquering Depression, *published by Doubleday, 1994.*

our brain chemistry is unique and responds differently to different medications. It may take trying more than one medication to get the right antidepressant for any given person. Also, the dosages may need to be altered for proper effectiveness. Communicate that it is important for group members to be educated about depression and medication as there are many myths surrounding this subject.

4. *Many group members suffer from the "pull yourself up by the bootstraps" syndrome and may feel ashamed of their depression.*
It is important to recognize that some women will suffer alone with their depression and will experience self-hatred related to their depression. As a facilitator, you can address some of the shame of depression by validating a person's feelings, helping members see the commonality of this issue for women, and by talking about how abuse and depression are connected. (In some of our groups, the majority of women have been on antidepressant medication.) It is essential that you communicate to the group that women needn't suffer alone or try to overcome depression by themselves. Help is available to address depression; depression need not ruin a person's life.

5. *Perfectionism, unrealistic expectations, abusive and punitive self-directed statements, overachievement, lack of permission to feel, and a competitive lifestyle could all be related to depression in some circumstances.*
Be aware of the negative family-of-origin messages and the "shoulds" and "oughts" that may lead to these lifestyle problems and depression. Talk about how loud our internal voices can become when we see ourselves as not good enough or less than other people. Talk about how self-acceptance is a key to dealing with depression. But self-acceptance is difficult when another person, such as an abusive partner, or other situations in our lives lead us to feel badly about ourselves.

Notes, comments, and observations:

Cluster 5

Looking Towards the Future

Self-Care

Goals

In this session, participants will:

1. Explore needs related to self-care.

2. Understand how energy for self-care is depleted in abusive relationships.

3. Identify consequences of neglecting self-care.

4. Develop a plan for self-care.

5. Recognize self-love as an important concept.

Format

Self-care for women has traditionally not been encouraged in our culture. In fact, just the opposite may be true. It seems that women have been taught to regard their own needs as secondary to those of their partners and children. Women who put themselves first have often been seen as uncaring and selfish. In this session, the importance of self-care will be considered.

1. Check-In

2. Self-Care Needs

Self-care is a concept that may be somewhat foreign to many women. This may be particularly true for group members who are in abusive relationships. Begin this session by asking what self-care is or what it means to group members. Suggest that self-care can be viewed in many different ways, but that to begin with in this session it will be considered in terms of physical, emotional, and intellectual needs. Ask the group for their ideas and include some of the following ideas (write on the chalkboard):

Self-Care Needs

Physical	*Emotional*	*Intellectual*
Rest	Friends	Challenges
Relaxation	Support	Knowledge
Positive environment	Fun	Outside work/activity
Exercise	Alone time	Education
Proper nutrition	Stress management	Time to think
Good appearance	Self-love	Being creative

Talk about how each person has a limited supply of energy to be used and distributed throughout the day. At some point, that energy level is depleted and sleep is necessary to rebuild the supply. When a woman is living in an abusive relationship, a great deal of energy is spent on trying to stay safe and keeping her children safe.

Consequently, it is all too easy to neglect personal self-care needs, as thoughts and energy are frequently focused elsewhere. Also, abusive partners may try to thwart or prevent a group member's participation in meeting some of her self-care needs. For example, a partner may believe he has the right to decide with whom she can be friends, whether or not she has a job outside of the home, or if she can pursue an education. Sometimes it is difficult for a group member to see how she neglects her personal self-care when she is in an abusive relationship, and there is little or no encouragement for her to recognize her own needs.

3. Consequences of Neglecting Self-Care

Ask the group to talk about the negative results of neglecting self-care needs. Ask them to think about what a typical day is like in their abusive relationship and how the abuse has affected their health, self-esteem, confidence, social life, energy level, household tasks, and parenting. Also discuss the impact of not recognizing the need for self-care. Encourage them to think about the importance of self-care, particularly its impact on their inner self.

4. Self-Care Planning

Next, pass out copies of the self-care plan worksheet and the sample plan (Appendix G, pages 188–189). Suggest briefly reviewing the sample plan to get an idea of how to formulate a personalized self-care plan. Allow ten to fifteen minutes to complete this exercise.

When plans are completed, ask each member to respond to the following:

- Share something specific in your plan
- Share something you learned about yourself
- Identify one self-care need you plan to begin working on in the next week

Ask the group to report during check-in next week on their progress in meeting self-care needs they agreed to work on.

5. Self-Love

Last, talk about self-love and how it relates to self-care. Suggest that it is important to love ourselves and be good to ourselves in order to care for and nurture others in our lives. Remind the group that in our culture, women are socialized to put others first and themselves second. Talk about the damage this does to a group member's sense of herself as a separate and important being. Suggest that self-love involves allowing oneself to develop, to trust, to be, to praise, to create, to reward, to forgive, to allow, and to empower oneself.

> **Break**

6. Individual Time-Taking

7. Closing

Issues

1. *Self-care needs to be on a conscious level.*
   Group members will usually take some steps towards self-care on their own but will not necessarily recognize or identify them as such. Members may need help to identify the need for self-care in different areas and to start the process of nurturing themselves in this way. The identification process will help self-care become a more conscious activity.

2. *Most women are socialized to take care of the needs of others before their own.*
   In our Western culture, women are usually trained to be the primary caregivers, nurturers, and caretakers of others. Often this includes male partners as well as children. Caring for others first may be a disservice to women, as they have difficulty learning to care for themselves appropriately and see themselves as worthwhile and deserving of good self-care. Encourage group members to think about what rights and needs they may have as individuals. Suggest that their needs should come first some of the time.

3. *Group members will be accused of being selfish for tending to self-care needs.*
   This is a common experience for women, and abusive partners will sometimes accuse a woman of being lazy, incompetent, a bad mother, selfish, uncaring, and neglectful for meeting some of her own needs. This hurts deeply and can make her feel ashamed of doing things for herself. It often contributes to her denying self-care needs and doubling efforts to care for her abusive partner. Encourage group members to see the trap in this thinking and the futility of increasing their caretaking of others.

4. *Partners may intimidate group members into altering or changing self-care plans.*
   When a group member begins to take steps toward a self-care plan, her abusive partner may become threatened and feel he is losing control. A partner may sabotage her plans or insist that she drop her self-care plan to

tend to him or the family. Help group members to recognize this so that if or when it happens, they can see it for what it is rather than view themselves as bad or wrong.

5. *A self-care plan must take into consideration the safety factor in an abusive relationship.*
   Remind group members that *safety* is always their first consideration when deciding how to implement a self-care plan. If meeting a friend may result in physical harm, they must consider how best to protect themselves in this or any given situation. Encourage group members to trust their instincts to make good, safe, self-care decisions.

6. *Family and friends may be negative about self-care needs and plans.*
   Some group members have family members and friends who feel threatened when a woman starts to take steps to care for herself. They will put her down, be unsupportive, accuse her of being selfish, and generally communicate disapproval. This can have a powerful effect on a group member if it causes her to feel she isn't pleasing people, something women are often trained to do. It's another Catch-22 for her because she does not want to be without those people who are supposed to care for her, nor does she want to be under their control. Recognizing this dilemma may help a group member find a way to balance her self-care needs.

7. *Small and consistent steps are the key to a successful self-care plan.*
   Encourage group members not to put a self-care plan into motion all at once. Talk about how to avoid becoming overwhelmed and say that a self-care plan should feel good for and to them. Suggest that taking small and careful steps is a positive way to begin. Celebrate successes as progress is made in the plan for good self-care.

Notes, comments, and observations:

Healthy Relationships

Goals

In this session, participants will:

1. Identify what they would *like* in a relationship and compare that to what they are *getting* in a relationship.

2. Increase their awareness of what constitutes healthy versus unhealthy relationships.

3. Better understand the differences in how women take responsibility for others in healthy and unhealthy ways.

Format

Women who are abused often come to believe that healthy relationships do not exist. They know how power and control work and begin to take on negative, stereotypical views of men. This session will look at what is healthy and unhealthy in a relationship and what group members can do to seek healthy relationships.

1. Check-In

2. What I Want in a Healthy Relationship

Begin this session by communicating that although there are many different kinds of relationships, this session will be focusing on partner relationships. For those group members who are no longer in a relationship with their abusive partner, suggest that they think back to the abusive relationship or think of a current relationship as they participate in this session.

Pass out a sheet of paper (or have each person create a sheet) that looks like this:

What I want in a relationship with my partner.

1. _____   6. _____

2. _____   7. _____

3. _____   8. _____

4. _____   9. _____

5. _____   10. _____

Ask group members to take five minutes to fill this out. As a facilitator, you can also participate in completing this exercise.

Next ask each group member to share her list with the group.

As the participants do this, track frequent similarities of wants on the chalkboard. Briefly point out the relationship wants that many members have in common. Now ask each member to go back and circle the qualities on her list that she feels she is currently getting in the relationship with her partner. (Those group members not in a relationship can think about their past relationship as they complete the exercise.) Ask each member to share the number of qualities she circled and identify them. Finally, as a group, discuss the discrepancies between the desired qualities and those that are actually present in their relationships. Ask how it feels to hear these differences.

Write the following on the chalkboard:

Relationships

You + Me + Relationship = Healthy

You + Me = Relationship = Unhealthy

Discuss the idea that healthy relationships involve three components: (1) you, (2) your partner, and (3) the relationship. Each needs care and consideration and should be nurtured separately and independently of the others. When any one of these three is neglected or left out of the healthy relationship equation, there is a potential for trouble. The equation for an unhealthy relationship omits the need to care for and nurture the individuals as separate entities, because they don't really exist outside the relationship. In the unhealthy equation, "you" and "me" constitutes the relationship rather than the relationship being separate. "You" and "me" and the "relationship" are all enmeshed with each other. Now, write on the chalkboard:

Healthy versus *Unhealthy*

Ask the group to brainstorm what healthy and unhealthy characteristics in a relationship might look like. Help them find the comparable opposite to fill out both the healthy and unhealthy characteristics. Some of the healthy characteristics will be wants from the list they just created.

Here is a sample list to help you guide the group in this exercise:

Healthy versus	*Unhealthy*
Trust	Deceit, dishonesty
Problem-solve	Fight, avoid
Encourage	Undermine
Take responsibility for own actions	Blame, belittle other
Listen, hear	Ignore, talk over
Respect	Disrespect
Fairness	Power and control
Give (in balance)	Take (out of balance)
Spend quality time together	Too busy, uninterested in partner
Win/win	Win/lose or lose/lose
Acknowledge feelings	Discount feelings
Safety	Fear/anxiety
Share intimacy, affection	No closeness, withdrawal
Negotiate	Lack of cooperation
Open and honest communication	Silent treatment
Pleasurable sex	Obligatory or unwanted sex

Ask the group to discuss how they feel about this list. (Note: Some of the characteristics overlap or are interchangeable.)

3. Healthy versus Unhealthy Responsibility

Finally, tell the group that they will carry the healthy versus unhealthy relationships one step further by talking about what women do when they feel responsible "for" others versus "to" others. Write the following on the board and ask the group members to brainstorm their ideas.

When I Feel Responsible . . .		
"For" others I . . . versus		*"To" others I . . .*
Fix		Nurture
Rescue		Encourage
Control		Let go
Don't listen		Listen
Am "right"		Am sensitive
Manipulate		Acknowledge
Discount feelings		Validate
Blame		Confront gently
Project		Express feelings
Assume		Help, guide
Attack		Trust

Ask if these two lists could be labeled unhealthy and healthy as well. Discuss how easy it is to begin feeling responsible "for" others when in an abusive relationship, and the negative impact that has on women. Ask each group member to pick out one thing from the "for others" list to change and from the "to others" list to practice doing. Plan to report about how this went in next week's check-in.

Remind the group members that if they tend to take responsibility "for" others versus "to" others, they are not bad or wrong. Rather, this is a reflection of the confusion of dealing with abuse and unhealthy relationships. Sometimes an abused woman and her children must fix, control, or manipulate just to survive.

> **Break**

4. Individual Time Taking

5. Closing

Issues

1. *Group members may be discouraged when they understand how few of their relationship needs and wants are being met.*
   This is particularly true for group members who are currently in an abusive relationship. They will report getting somewhere from zero to two of their "wants" list. The reality of their personal relationships can be discouraging.

2. *Group members may question whether healthy relationships are even possible.*
   Some group members believe that healthy relationships are highly unlikely, if not impossible, because there are so few nonabusive and mature men. Take this opportunity to talk about this belief as a myth. Help group members see that not all men are abusive and that healthy relationships are not impossible. Also, suggest they can explore this further in the Questions about Men Who Batter session.

3. *The identity of some group members has suffered in the abusive relationship.*
   Some group members will take on the identity of their partner or the relationship to cope with the abuse. They will try to think like their partner, take on their partner's values, and become what their partner indicates is desirable in a woman. It is more difficult for women with blurred identities to comprehend the three relationship entities and how they need nurturing and separate attention.

Notes, comments, and observations:

Evaluating New Relationships

Goals

In this session, participants will:

1. Discuss readiness for, and expectations of, new relationships.

2. Explore ways to evaluate new relationships.

3. Discuss the importance of knowing and stating needs at the outset in new relationships.

4. Identify early warning signs of abuse in potential new relationships.

5. Become aware of the importance of considering signs of abuse before committing themselves to a new relationship.

Format

New relationships are exciting, fun, and often make us feel especially alive again. Being in love is a great place to be and somehow we want to believe that we will be there forever. But reality creeps in, and women *need* to take a good look at the person with whom they are involving themselves. This session will focus on evaluating a new relationship to make sure it will not be hurtful or abusive.

1. Check-In

2. Expectations

Open a discussion by asking some of the following questions:

- Are you ready for a new relationship?

- Have you addressed the pain of the last relationship?

- Are you expecting that a new partner will be the key to your happiness? Is this realistic?

- Could you be happy and content without being in a relationship?

- Are you looking for another person to solve all your problems?
- How would you approach a new relationship?

3. Evaluating New Relationships

Explore ways to evaluate if a potential new relationship is nonabusive. Suggest that it is *extremely important* for group members to be themselves and state their needs in the early stages of the relationship. Group members must pay attention to how their needs and wants are received. This is important because many group members have a tendency to quickly become involved in a relationship that is difficult to back away from when red flags begin to appear. If needs are stated from the outset, early evaluation can begin to determine if this relationship is safe and if needs will be respected.

Ask the group to think about ways to evaluate a new partner and how he treats women. Write *Evaluating a New Partner for Abuse* on the chalkboard and add any of the following ideas to those of the group:

- Does he lack understanding of your personal schedule and obligations?
- What is his behavior like around his male friends when he is with you?
- What is his perception of gender equality? Does he need to be dominant?
- Does he give gifts to apologize for bad behavior?
- Is he overly jealous of others in your life? Is he jealous of your children?
- Is he overly jealous of your ex-partner?
- What does he say about the abuse you have suffered?
- Is he suspicious of what you are doing when you are not with him?
- Consider his boundaries. Does he help himself to things in your home without asking your permission? Does he begin to move his things into your home (clothes, etc.) without asking?
- Does he try to tell you where you can go and what you can do?
- Are you afraid of his anger? Does he have a short fuse?
- Does he want you to give or loan him money?
- Does he push for quick and exclusive involvement?

Communicate to the group that any one thing on this list may not necessarily indicate an abusive man but that several early warning signs added together might cause a woman to consider possible red flags in this new relationship. Have a volunteer write down the ideas to hand out at the next session.

4. Early Warning Signs

Ask the group members who are in a new relationship or considering a new relationship to add up those signs on the chalkboard to evaluate a new partner they are considering. Ask that they share the number with the group. Ask each person how soon in the relationship she began to see some of the early warning signs. Ask if they felt they were committed to the relationship and were unwilling to detach from it before the signs were apparent to them. Stress how very important it is for a group member to state her needs and wants early in the relationship and evaluate whether these needs and wants are respected by the new partner. The timing of this is important because it must be done before the feelings are so strong that the relationship can't be easily broken off.

Pass out copies of the worksheet in Appendix G, page 190. Ask each member to take a few minutes to fill it out. Suggest that she think back to past or current relationships to recall some of the early warning signs that existed but were either ignored or not given sufficient weight. She should write down these ideas or thoughts along with any of the warning signs on the chalkboard that she thinks might be important for her to consider as she enters a new relationship.

Ask each person to share her list. Suggest that they add to their lists any ideas they hear that might be helpful to them as the lists are shared by their group peers. Now ask each group member who is currently evaluating a new relationship how she might want to address one or two early warning signs in the relationship. Ask if she could do this in the next week and report to the group on the results of her efforts.

5. Living without a Partner

Summarize this session by talking about the idea of experiencing life as a woman without a partner or a relationship for a period of time. Ask the group some of the following questions:

- Has anyone considered being without a partner and not dating for one year or longer?
- What positives might come from not being involved in a dating relationship for a period of time?
- How could this enhance a woman's self-esteem?
- How might doing this affect future choices in a partner?
- How have women been socialized to believe they must be in a relationship to be worthwhile?

Lastly, ask the group what they got from this session that might help them avoid an unhealthy relationship or another abusive partner. Go around the group for each person's comments.

Break

6. Individual Time Taking

7. Closing

Issues

1. *Only some of the group members will be in a new relationship or considering a new relationship.*
   Generally, this session topic will not be chosen unless it is relevant to half or more of the group members. If it is selected as a topic, you will need to make some adjustments for the members who do not particularly relate to this topic. Suggest that the group members who are with their abusive partners and not considering future relationships think back to the beginning of their relationship and respond to the session from that perspective.

2. *Record the ideas that are presented for evaluating a new partner.*
   This is an important list for group members to have for future reference. Be sure someone records these ideas along with some of the ideas from the guidebook, to be typed and distributed at the next session. Ask the group to hang on to this list for future reference.

3. *Expect the group to contribute more obvious, overt early warning signals.*
   These might include threatening behaviors, criminal involvement, and alcohol or drug issues. You can suggest some of the more subtle signs that group members may not think about or be aware of at this time. Many are included in the Evaluating a New Partner list.

4. *Some women will become involved in a new relationship while still with their abusive partner.*
   Some group members will share with the group that they have become involved with a new man, and others will want to keep this a secret. The subject can be delicate, and group members may become judgmental. Usually, though, group members are supportive and concerned more with the safety of the involved group member. Point out that one of the ways women address the loneliness in an abusive relationship is to become attracted to another person. However, this may not be the best way to address or solve the problems of an abusive relationship. Once again, the major concern is for the woman's safety and providing a safe place for her to think through what is happening.

5. *Some group members believe that all men are abusive and that there are no good men available with whom to form new relationships.*
   As a facilitator, you can state that you do not believe this to be true. You can talk about your own or a friend's or relative's healthy and respectful relationship. Suggest that one of the reasons some group members believe there are no good men is that abusive relationships are the only experiences they have known. When equipped with more information about abuse, they find it easier to avoid future abusive or hurtful relationships. Healthier partners may become more apparent, and abusive partners may be more quickly discovered and rejected.

6. *Some group members have been in partner relationships their entire adult life.*
   It has never even occurred to some group members to experience life without a male partner. You could introduce the idea of considering a period of time without a dating relationship or a partnership. Talk about the

potential positives of a healing time, a time for self-reflection, a time to think about what they want in a relationship. Time alone can be very exciting and empowering for group members and can be an opportunity to become more clear about future choices.

Notes, comments, and observations:

Cluster 6

Closure to the Group

Closing Session

Goals

In this session, participants will:

1. Increase informal social skills and celebrate accomplishments.
2. Identify a plan for ongoing support.
3. Listen to and begin to integrate individual personal strengths.
4. Review personal group goals and identify progress related to these goals.
5. Increase awareness of the importance of a closure process.

Format

The closing session is a celebration of the accomplishments of the group and a final closure to the group process. It usually includes food and special activities that are designed to affirm group members. It is usually an emotional time for the group members as they say their good-byes to women with whom they have developed strong bonds.

Pre-Planning for the Closing Session

As you approach the final stage of the group process, talk about the last session as being different from all the other sessions. Tell the group that it will be a time to celebrate accomplishments and to say good-bye. It will be an uplifting time together and a time to express many different feelings.

Most groups decide to have a potluck supper (or order pizza) at the closing session. Plan this in advance; one member can be in charge of organizing this event. One or two weeks before the last session, prepare a sign-up sheet for what each person wants to bring. Group facilitators need not be involved in food preparation unless they wish to be.

Tell the group at the preceding session that the first thing on the agenda for this session will be to set up the potluck food and eat together.

1. Celebrating Group Accomplishments

Once the eating has started and the group circle is in place, ask the members to check in. After check-in is completed, introduce an informal conversation about what has been accomplished in the group. This is a good time to reminisce and share memories.

2. Ongoing Support Planning

Begin to talk about what group members' plans are for ongoing support for the future. Go around the group, asking each person what her thoughts and plans are to care for herself and to get support related to her issues of abuse.

If your program has its own aftercare or continuing-care program, talk about that option in detail. Invite a facilitator or member of the aftercare group to talk to your group. Include in your discussion the day, time, cost (if any), child-care availability, and the general group format. If this type of group is not available as ongoing support, be prepared to offer community resources as possible options. Tell group members that some private therapists have women's support groups that can be helpful and that usually there will be a cost for these. Also, many battered women's shelters offer no-cost women's support groups that are open to nonresidents of the shelter. Ask members to share any other ideas they have for ongoing support.

Suggest a very short break for a brief cleanup since time is important.

Break

3. Identify Individual Strengths

After everyone has returned to the group circle, tell about the strengths exercise that the group will be doing. Hand out the worksheet Your Strengths (see Appendix G, page 191). Tell the group that each person will have an opportunity to listen to what the group sees as her individual strengths. Each group member will be on the hot seat while the rest of the group describes her strengths and the facilitator records them on the worksheet. Members will be given this list to take home and keep in a safe place so they can frequently remind themselves of what their group peers see as their strengths.

Ask for a volunteer to begin the process. If no one volunteers, choose someone. Request that the person on the hot seat not talk but listen and take in what her group peers say about her. This is a difficult assignment, and as a facilitator, you may need to continue encouraging group members to hear what people are saying. As the exercise is in progress, expect and allow some silences or pauses as people think of what they want to say.

Allow about five minutes per person for the group to brainstorm an individual person's strengths. After the list is completed, ask the person on the hot seat how it felt to hear her strengths as seen by her group peers. Give her the list and request that she read it back to the group. Ask her where she can keep it in her home that it will be safe and available to refer to often. As the exercise proceeds, ask each member to choose another member to go next. Group facilitators should be included in this exercise, but will go last.

Next, pass out the Goals and Strengths worksheet (Appendix F, page 179) that was completed at the intake for each group member some four months earlier. It is fun for group members to see what their thoughts were that long ago. This should be a brief exercise because lack of time is almost always an issue in this final session. Ask members to comment on how the strengths they saw in themselves four months ago compare to how they see their strengths today. Ask them to comment on the progress they've made on the goals that they set at the start of the program.

4. Final Good-byes

Hopefully, you now have twenty to thirty minutes of time remaining to say the final good-byes. Tell the group that each member will have a few minutes to say whatever she wants for her good-bye and closure. She may want to talk about what the group has meant to her, how it feels to say goodbye, or any other more specific good-byes to other group members. As the facilitator, you will need to encourage a time limit.

Finally, it is nice to have a reading to close the group. We suggest that group members bring poems to be read; we also keep a collection of poems that can be distributed. Ask group members to read the poems aloud. After final cleanup and more informal good-byes, the group has come to an end.

Issues

1. *Time is limited for the final closing session agenda.*
   There is usually more to do than time allows at this session. Safeguard the time schedule with careful planning. Encourage group members to arrive a little early so that any food preparation or setup is completed by the designated starting time of group. Suggest that the break after eating be rather brief so that at least ninety to one-hundred minutes remain for closing exercises. If necessary, eliminate the review of individual goals to allow plenty of time for the personal closure and good-byes.

2. *Individual time taking is not an agenda item in the final session.*
   It is best to announce this at the preceding session so group members are not expecting time taking to occur. If a woman is in crisis or requests individual time to work through issues with the group, do what you can to structure it in, or offer an individual session in the next few days.

3. *Final group evaluations that are incomplete should be finished at this session.*
   It is a good idea to have the group complete the final evaluations (Appendix G, pages 183–184) at the fifteenth session, when there is more time to devote to this.

   If any group members were absent at the preceding session when group evaluations were filled out, encourage that the evaluations be completed at this final session. Try to catch those group members before the group begins, so they can fill in an evaluation during the first part of the session. It is important to have the entire group's attention for the closing exercises after the break. If you send evaluations home, you are not likely to get them back.

4. ***The socializing time while sharing a meal is sometimes awkward.***
Up until this session, group members have had a structure provided for them at every step of the way. Suddenly they are in a social situation that is less structured and is intimate in a new and different way by virtue of dining together. This can lead to silent pauses and unsure feelings. Come prepared with some ideas for conversation to help with any awkward moments.

5. ***Group members will often talk about reunion meetings.***
Suggest to the group that this is a great idea and that they may need a person to commit herself to organizing this. The group will often assume that the leaders can be a part of the reunion. You will need to gently tell them that this is not possible for several reasons. Explain that you are not able to socialize with participants outside of the program structure. Also, tell them that you will likely be facilitating another group during this time period. If your facility can accommodate their reunion meeting in the future, suggest that you could drop in to greet them if time allows.

6. ***The strengths exercise is powerful and has the potential to raise a number of issues.***
   (a) A facilitator should record the list of strengths for each person; sometimes asking group members to do this imposes a risk of embarrassment over poor spelling or illegible writing.

   (b) Sometimes the strengths are stated at such a rapid pace that facilitators can't keep up with recording them. Ask the group members to give you time to catch up.

   (c) Group members have a tendency to look at the person recording the strengths as they state them. Ask group members to look at the woman on the hot seat and tell her directly what they see as her strengths.

   (d) Group members often feel embarrassed about hearing good things about themselves, using laughter and joking to cover up embarrassment. While you certainly want to allow some of this, encourage the person not to talk and instead to take in the good things being said about her and to her.

   (e) Group members can become emotional and feel overwhelmed at hearing so many nice things all at once. Be prepared for these feelings and process them as needed.

   (f) A group member may have difficulty reading the list back to the group because of powerful feelings. If she is unable to continue reading, ask if she would like another group member to read the list for her.

   (g) Sometimes a group member will state that she has a hard time believing that the strengths stated to her are true. You might ask if she trusts the group to be honest with her. Also, you might suggest that women are often used to being put down and that it is not easy to hear the positive things being said to them.

(h) Sometimes strengths are stated that do not sound positive. Encourage the group to help restate meanings into positive language.

(i) Strength lists will vary in length. Communicate to the group that with each additional person in the hot seat, the group gets better at thinking of strengths.

(j) It is important to include the facilitators in this exercise because the group members truly want a chance to express what they see in the facilitators as well as in each other.

(k) Silences will occur as people are thinking. There is a danger that the person on the hot seat will interpret this to mean she lacks strengths. Assure the group at the beginning that this is not the case and that thinking time is needed in this exercise.

7. ***Address future contact by group members with you or your program/agency.*** Clarify what future services you or your program can make available to group members. If possible, offer an individual closing session as an option to each group member. Some members want this opportunity while others are ready to move on without it. Suggest that group members can call if they have any questions about the group or the group process. Try to communicate what you can realistically provide in the future without encouraging frequent contact.

Notes, comments, and observations:

Appendices

Appendix A:
Group Definitions of Abuse

A power imbalance is inherent in the experience of any and all forms of abuse.

PHYSICAL

Hitting
Punching
Pushing
Kicking
Restraining and holding
Biting
Choking
Threatening with
  weapons
Hair pulling
Grabbing
Destroying property
Threatening with fist

Throwing things at you
Practicing martial arts
  to intimidate
Scratching
Slapping
Reckless driving
Pushing you out of car
Poking
Taking car keys
Touching with control
Banging against a wall
Thrown around bodily
Excessive tickling

VERBAL

Name calling
Swearing
Yelling
Degrading comments
Mimicking
Threatening to take
  children away
Put-downs
Lying/deceitfulness
Brainwashing
Sarcasm
Outright cruelty
Using information you
  have revealed against
  you

Blaming
Guilt-producing
  statements
"You are not okay"
  statements
Demanding
Threatening tone of
  voice
Contradicting
Irrational questioning
Interrogating
Twisting your words
Calling you "crazy"

SEXUAL

Forcing sex
Withholding sex
Rude stories/gestures
Double standards
Using sex as a weapon
Punishment for not
  complying
Making sexual threats
  with objects
Talking dirty
Laughing at you
Shaming

Intimidation to do
  unwanted acts
  outside of comfort
  level
Sex as form of control
Sexualizing in public
Rape
Possessiveness
Mocking of body parts
Accusations
Sex for favors
Pornography

EMOTIONAL

Double standards
Crazy-making behaviors
Isolation from family/
  friends
Silent treatment
Accusations
Twisting things
Telling you how you
  feel and think
"His" agenda
Avoiding issues
Tension in home
Immature behavior
Sabotaging
Bringing up past
Playing mind games

Withholding money
Inequity in the
  partnership
Harming pets
Questioning paternity
Selective memory
Controlling the money
Stalking
Harassing
Degrading in public
Not okay to be sick
Intimidation
Discounting behaviors
Threatening suicide
Empty promises
Guilty gift-giving

Appendix B:
What Keeps Women in Abusive Relationships

1. Guilt
2. Children want a dad/pressure from children
3. Money/financial problems without him
4. Companionship
5. Upbringing modeled abuse as normal
6. Hope it's going to improve/hope he'll change
7. History together
8. Commitment to relationship
9. Don't want to look/feel like a failure
10. Don't want to divorce
11. Loneliness
12. Fear of living alone or being alone
13. Not wanting to look for someone else
14. Fear of losing children
15. Not wanting to grieve
16. Threats of harm
17. Fear of physical harm
18. Fear of losing house, car
19. Pressure from others
20. Feeling defective
21. Low self-esteem
22. Preserving reputation as a family
23. Self-blame for the abuse
24. Single parenting is unattractive
25. Left out of social functions/invitations
26. Stigma/rejection
27. Love him
28. Sex
29. Affection, kindness, touch, some of the time
30. Promises
31. Apologies/crying
32. Security
33. Losing his family
34. Cycle is familiar
35. Not wanting to start over
36. Not wanting to give up "the dream"
37. Threats of suicide by him
38. His power/his family's power
39. Social status
40. Religion
41. Fear of harassment
42. "Mr. Nice Guy" image
43. Fear of the unknown
44. Lack of awareness that it's okay to leave
45. Not identifying what is going on as abuse
46. Feeling of not being wanted by anyone else
47. No support system
48. Nowhere to go
49. Others blame you
50. Learn to think certain behaviors are normal
51. No one may believe you

Appendix C: Feelings Vocabulary

Emotional signals are the feelings you have before, during, or after the times that you have been abused. There are names for these signals. "Angry" or "upset" are the easy ones. Try to identify the most exact name for the feeling you have had by looking at the list of feelings under the category for that feeling.

HAPPY	SAD		CONFUSED	ANGRY	SCARED
Excited	Regretful	Empty	Bewildered	Strangled	Fearful
Elated	Islanded	Miserable	Trapped	Furious	Panicky
Exuberant	Resigned	Distraught	Immobilized	Seething	Afraid
Ecstatic	Drained	Deserted	Directionless	Enraged	Shocked
Terrific	Slighted	Grief stricken	Stagnant	Hostile	Overwhelmed
Jubilant	Degraded	Burdened	Flustered	Vengeful	Intimidated
Enthusiastic	Deprived	Demoralized	Baffled	Incensed	Desperate
Loved	Disturbed	Condemned	Constricted	Abused	Frantic
Thrilled	Wasted	Terrible	Troubled	Hateful	Terrified
Uplifted	Abandoned	Unwanted	Ambivalent	Humiliated	Vulnerable
Marvelous	Sorry	Unloved	Awkward	Sabotaged	Horrified
Justified	Lost	Mournful	Puzzled	Betrayed	Petrified
Valued	Bad	Pitiful	Disorganized	Repulsed	Appalled
Gratified	Disenchanted	Discarded	Foggy	Rebellious	Full of dread
Encouraged	Deflated	Disgraced	Perplexed	Pissed off	Tormented
Optimistic	Apathetic	Disheartened	Hesitant	Outraged	Tense
Joyful	Devastated	Despised	Torn	Fuming	Threatened
Proud	Hopeless	Disappointed	Misunderstood	Exploited	Uneasy
Cheerful	Sorrowful	Upset	Doubtful	Throttled	Defensive
Relieved	Depressed	Inadequate	Bothered	Mad	Insecure
Assured	Wounded	Dismal	Undecided	Spiteful	Skeptical
Determined	Hurt	Unappreciated	Uncomfortable	Patronized	Apprehensive
Grateful	Drained	Discouraged	Uncertain	Vindictive	Suspicious
Appreciated	Defeated	Ashamed	Surprised	Used	Alarmed
Confident	Exhausted	Distressed	Unsettled	Repulsed	Shaken
Respected	Helpless	Distant	Unsure	Ridiculed	Swamped
Admired	Crushed	Disillusioned	Distracted	Resentful	Startled
Accepted	Worthless	Lonely		Disgusted	Guarded
Amused	Uncared for	Neglected		Smothered	Stunned
Delighted	Dejected	Isolated		Frustrated	Awed
Alive	Rejected	Alienated		Stifled	Reluctant
Fulfilled	Humbled			Offended	Anxious
Tranquil				Controlled	Impatient
Content				Peeved	Shy
Relaxed				Annoyed	Nervous
Glad				Agitated	Unsure
Good				Irritated	Timid
Satisfied				Exasperated	Concerned
Peaceful				Harassed	Perplexed
Hopeful				Anguished	Doubtful
Fortunate				Deceived	
Pleased				Aggravated	
Flattered				Perturbed	
				Provoked	
				Dominated	
				Coerced	
				Cheated	
				Uptight	
				Dismayed	
				Tolerant	
				Displeased	

Appendix D:
Women's Intake Questionnaire[10]

Now, I'd like you to think about the relationship which brought you to the Women's Domestic Abuse Program. Please think back over this relationship. I'm going to read a list of things your partner might have done to you during your relationship. Using a scale from 1 to 5, where 1 = Never, 2 = Rarely, 3 = Sometimes, 4 = Often, and 5 = All the time, please indicate how often your partner did these things to you.

	Never	Rarely	Sometimes	Often	All the time	Not applicable
a. Yelled at you	1	2	3	4	5	9
b. Refused to talk to you	1	2	3	4	5	9
c. Withdrew affection	1	2	3	4	5	9
d. Called you names	1	2	3	4	5	9
e. Slapped you	1	2	3	4	5	9
f. Tried to intimidate you with looks (for example, stares, glares)	1	2	3	4	5	9
g. Threatened to hit you	1	2	3	4	5	9
h. Swore at you	1	2	3	4	5	9
i. Pushed you	1	2	3	4	5	9
j. Hit you	1	2	3	4	5	9
k. Grabbed you	1	2	3	4	5	9
l. Threw something at you	1	2	3	4	5	9
m. Bit you	1	2	3	4	5	9
n. Controlled major decisions (for example, where to live, use of car, money)	1	2	3	4	5	9
o. Made verbal threats to harm you	1	2	3	4	5	9
p. Kicked you	1	2	3	4	5	9
q. Restricted your social contacts	1	2	3	4	5	9
r. Punched you	1	2	3	4	5	9
s. Choked you	1	2	3	4	5	9

[10] *This intake questionnaire is adapted from materials developed by Murray E. Straus of the The University of New Hampshire, Durham. Used with permission.*

Appendix D: Women's Intake Questionnaire (continued)

		Never	Rarely	Sometimes	Often	All the time	Not applicable
t.	Destroyed property	1	2	3	4	5	9
u.	Threatened to take the children away from you	1	2	3	4	5	9
v.	Threatened you with a weapon (for example, knife, gun, other object)	1	2	3	4	5	9
w.	Verbally pressured you to have sex	1	2	3	4	5	9
x.	Physically forced you to have sex	1	2	3	4	5	9
y.	Threatened to kill you	1	2	3	4	5	9
z.	Degraded you sexually (for example, made you the object of dirty jokes, forced you to look at pornography, threatened you sexually with objects)	1	2	3	4	5	9

Appendix E:
Women's Domestic Abuse Summary Sheet

Date: _____

Name: _____

Partner's or Ex-Partner's Name: _____

Who currently lives with you? _____

How long have you been/were you in this relationship? _____

Children's Names	*Ages*	*Custody Status*

Referral source/other professionals working with you or your family:

_____

_____

_____

Describe the relationship or incident that brought you here:

Appendix E: Women's Domestic Abuse Summary Sheet (page 2)

Name: _____

Talk about the abuse you have experienced in this relationship and what it has been like for you.

Do you have an Order For Protection?　yes _____　no _____

Have you experienced abuse in other adult relationships?

Do you have any concerns about your children?

Describe your family of origin (number of siblings, were your parents together, did people get along well or fight a lot). Were you abused as a child?

Appendix E: Women's Domestic Abuse Summary Sheet (page 3)

Name: _____

Do you have any concerns about your current chemical or drug use?
Have you ever been in chemical dependency treatment?

Do you feel you need assistance with any of your own behaviors that may be abusive? Please describe:

If things could be different for you, what would they look like?

Is there any other information that would be important for you to share today?

Appendix F:
Goals and Strengths

Goals I want to work on:

My strengths:

Signed _____

Appendix G:
Forms

Weekly Evaluation

1. How do you feel at the end of this week's group session?

2. What was the most helpful about this session?

3. What was the least helpful?

4. Did you get what you wanted for yourself in this session?

5. Other comments:

Mid-Term Evaluation

1. Overall, how satisfied have you been with this group so far? (Please circle one)

   Very Satisfied   **Somewhat Satisfied**   **Neutral**   **Somewhat Dissatisfied**   **Very Dissatisfied**

2. What do you find most helpful about the group?

3. What do you find least helpful about the group?

4. What suggestions do you have for improving the group?

5. If you were to tell someone else about this women's group, what would you say?

6. When you leave the group sessions, how do you usually feel?

7. What things would you like to see the group leader(s) do differently?

Final Evaluation

1. Considering the overall quality of this women's domestic abuse program, would you say it is:
   (Please circle one.)

   Excellent   **Very Good**   **Good**   **Fair**   **Poor**   **Very Poor**

2. Which of the following best describes how you feel about the help you have received? (Please circle one.)

   A Great Deal of Help   **Quite a Lot of Help**   **Some Help**   **A Little Help**   **No Help**

3. Compared to how you felt about yourself before starting this group, how do you feel now?
   (Please circle one.)

   Significantly Better   **Somewhat Better**   **About the Same**   **Somewhat Worse**   **Worse**

4. Would you recommend this program to other women? (Please circle)   Yes   No
   Please explain:

5. Did you usually complete or work on the sessions in your journal book?

   Was it helpful to write in the journal? Why or why not?

   What did you like best about the journal?

   What did you like least about the journal?

Final Evaluation (continued)

6. What was the single most important thing you learned in group?

Which group topic(s) were the most helpful for you in your particular circumstances?

7. What changes occurred in your life during the course of group related to your abusive experience? Were these changes positive or negative for you?

8. What suggestions do you have for improving the group?

9. Please list specific comments about the ability of the group leaders.

   Name: _____

   Name: _____

10. Please feel free to make any additional comments or suggestions.

House of Abuse

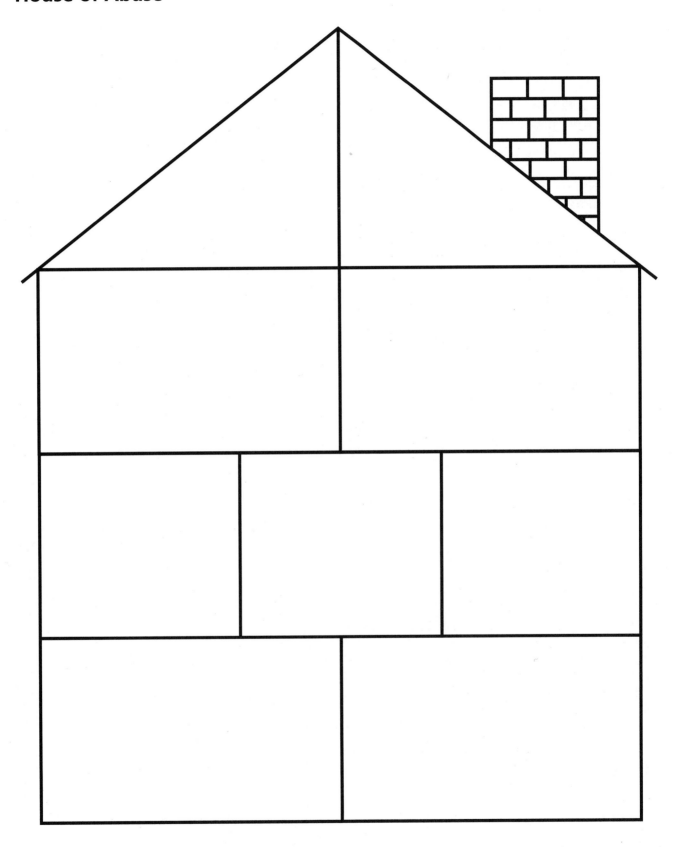

Emotional Abuse Checklist

Check the most appropriate answer.	Often	Sometimes	Rarely	Never
1. Do you have to get permission to socialize with your friends?				
2. Are you accused of cheating on him when you leave the house to do errands, etc.?				
3. Are you afraid to talk about certain topics unless he's in a good mood?				
4. Does he have control over the money and monitor your spending?				
5. Does he tell you no one else would ever want you?				
6. Does he threaten to harm himself if you leave him?				
7. Does he go through your purse or open your mail?				
8. Does he make disparaging remarks about the way you look or dress?				
9. Does he use things against you that you've confided to him in the past?				
10. Does he sabotage your efforts to be involved in pleasant social or family events?				
11. Does he compare you negatively to other women?				
12. Are you nervous about being on the phone when he is around?				
13. Is it okay to return home later than scheduled without being fearful?				
14. Does it feel more like you have a dad than a partner?				
15. Does he give you the "silent treatment" when you want to talk or work things out?				
16. Does he try to turn the children against you?				
17. Do you feel manipulated by his kindness or gifts?				
18. Do you feel obligated to be sexual with your partner?				
19. Are your activities and interests looked upon as unimportant and trivial?				
20. Does he sabotage your schedule and outside commitments?				

Assertiveness Situations

It is difficult for me to be assertive when . . . (circle all that apply to you)

1. Friends ask me to baby-sit.

2. People use their authority or position over me.

3. I want to return a purchase.

4. A salesperson puts pressure on me to buy.

5. Family/friends want extra favors.

6. I want time to myself.

7. Someone drops in unannounced and I am busy.

8. I am explaining about my strong points in a job interview.

9. People make hurtful/unkind remarks to me.

10. I am asked to take on additional work.

11. My partner demands I drop what I am doing to assist him.

12. My children want something *now*.

13. Tension is mounting in my home.

14. People around me are in a bad mood.

15. My partner wants to be sexual and I don't.

16. I need help from someone.

17. I feel sad and lonely.

18. I need support.

19. A problem arises that needs to be addressed.

20. What I have to say sounds like criticism.

21. Fill in the blank _____

22. Fill in the blank _____

Assertiveness Exercise

Assertiveness statement

When I feel _____

because of _____

I need to _____

and I want _____

Typical feelings: (examples)	Used	Selfish	Hurt
	Intimidated	Afraid/scared	Unworthy
	Embarrassed	Bothersome	Annoyed
	Boastful		

Assertiveness steps:

1. Identify the situation related to the assertiveness problem.

2. Identify the person related to the problem.

3. Develop a plan using the above assertiveness statement.

4. If appropriate, set a time and place with the person to accomplish this plan.

Sample Self-Care Plan

Needs	Currently Do	Would Like to Do	How/When
Physical			
1. Exercise	Nothing	Walk, yoga, bike ride	Use yoga video/early a.m.
2. Diet improvement	Snack too often	Reduce amount of snacks Eat low-fat snacks	Eat pretzels/2 times daily
3. Better appearance	Neglect hair	Get professional cut	Save $ for cuts/schedule monthly cuts
Emotional			
1. Self-love	Mental put-downs	Praise myself	Affirmations/daily
2. Manage stress	Can't say "no"	Assert myself more	Practice saying "no" when asked to baby-sit
3. Friendships	Avoid friends	Contact old friend	Call and make date/ next week
Intellectual			
1. Knowledge	Watch mindless TV	Watch learning channel, read a good book	Find a quiet spot/ after kids in bed
2. Creativity	Write letters	Design dress pattern	Sketch and draw/ early a.m.
3. Spiritual self	Pray	Meditate/commune with nature	Walking in the woods/ on the weekends

Self-Care Plan

Needs	Currently Do	Would Like to Do	How/When
Physical			
1.			
2.			
3.			
4.			
5.			
Emotional			
1.			
2.			
3.			
4.			
5.			
Intellectual			
1.			
2.			
3.			
4.			
5.			

Early Warning Signs

Possible warning signs I need to consider in a new relationship:

1. _____
   _____
   _____

2. _____
   _____
   _____

3. _____
   _____
   _____

4. _____
   _____
   _____

5. _____
   _____
   _____

6. _____
   _____
   _____

7. _____
   _____
   _____

8. _____
   _____
   _____

9. _____
   _____
   _____

10. _____
    _____
    _____

Your Strengths

Date: _____

_____ , we want you to know that we see the following strengths in you.
(Name)

1.

2.

3.

4.

5.

6.

7.

8.

9.

10.

Notes

Notes

Notes

Notes

Collaboration Handbook: Creating, Sustaining, and Enjoying the Journey

by Michael Winer and Karen Ray

Shows you how to get a collaboration going, define the results you're after, determine everyone's roles, create an action plan, and evaluate the results. Tells you what to expect and how to handle challenges in a way that strengthens your group. Includes a case study of one collaboration from start to finish, helpful tips on how to avoid pitfalls, and worksheets to keep everyone on track.

192 pages, softcover, $28.00

Collaboration: What Makes It Work

by Wilder Research Center

An in-depth review of current collaboration research in the health, social science, education, and public affairs fields. Major findings are summarized, critical conclusions drawn, and nineteen key factors influencing successful collaborations are identified. See if your collaboration's plans include the necessary ingredients.

53 pages, softcover, $14.00

Community Building: What Makes It Work

by Wilder Research Center

Shows you what really does (and doesn't) contribute to community building success. Reveals 28 keys to help you build community more effectively and efficiently. Includes detailed descriptions of each factor, case examples of how they play out, and practical questions you can use to assess your work.

112 pages, softcover, $20.00

Coping with Cutbacks (working title)

by Emil Angelica and Vincent Hyman

The welfare reform act of 1996 is just the tip of the iceberg. The partnership between nonprofits and the federal government is changing. This book helps you understand why and how this is occurring—and what you can do to prepare.

Marketing Workbook for Nonprofit Organizations Volume I: Develop the Marketing Plan

by Gary J. Stern

Don't just wish for results—get them! This book shows you how to create a straightforward, usable marketing plan. It includes the 6 P's of Marketing—and how to use them effectively—a sample marketing plan, and detachable worksheets.

132 pages, softcover, $25.00

Marketing Workbook for Nonprofit Organizations Volume II: Mobilize People for Marketing Success

by Gary J. Stern

Put together a successful promotional campaign based on the most persuasive tool of all: personal contact. This book shows you how to mobilize your entire organization, its staff, volunteers, and supporters in a focused, one-to-one marketing campaign. Provides step-by-step instructions, sample agendas for motivational trainings, and worksheets to keep the campaign organized and on track.

Also includes *Pocket Guide for Marketing Representatives,* a pocket guide available for all your representatives. In it, they can record key campaign messages and find motivational reminders.

208 pages, softcover, $25.00

Strategic Planning Workbook for Nonprofit Organizations, Revised and Updated

by Bryan Barry

Chart a wise course for your nonprofit's future. This time-tested workbook gives you practical step-by-step guidance, real-life examples, one nonprofit's complete strategic plan, and easy-to-use worksheets.

144 pages, softcover, $25.00

The Little Book of Peace

A pocket-size guide to help people think about violence and talk about it with their families and friends.

24 pages, .65 each (minimum order 10 copies)

What Works in Preventing Rural Violence

by Wilder Research Center

An in-depth review of 88 effective strategies to respond to rural violence. Also includes a Community Report Card with step-by-step directions on how you can collect, record, and use information about violence in your community.

94 pages, softcover, $17.00

Foundations for Violence-Free Living

A Step-by-Step Guide to Facilitating Men's Domestic Abuse Groups

by David J. Mathews, MA, LICSW

A complete guide to facilitating a men's domestic program. Includes 29 activities, detailed guidelines for presenting each activity, and a discussion of psychological issues that may arise out of each activity. Also gives you tips for intake, individual counseling, facilitating groups, working with resistant clients, and recommended policies and releases.

240 pages, softcover, $45.00

On the Level

(Participant's Workbook to Foundations for Violence-Free Living)

Contains 49 worksheets including midterm and final evaluations. Men can record their insights and progress. A permanent binding makes the workbook easy to carry home for outside assignments, and you don't have to make any trips to the copy machine.

160 pages, softcover, $15.00

Four easy ways to order

 Call toll-free: **1-800-274-6024**
8:00 am to 4:00 pm CST
(in Mpls./St. Paul: 612-659-6024)

 Fax order form to: **612-642-2061** (24 hours a day)

 Mail order form to: A. H. Wilder Foundation
Publishing Center
919 Lafond Avenue
St. Paul, MN 55104

 E-mail your order to: **books@wilder.org**

Shipping

Standard Charges:

If order totals:	Add:
Up to $30.00	$4.00
$30.01 - 60.00	$5.00
$60.01 - 150.00	$6.00
$150.01 - 500.00	$8.00
Over $500.00	3% of order

- Orders are shipped UPS or Parcel Post. Please allow two weeks for delivery.
- For orders outside the U.S. or Canada, please add an additional U.S. $5.00
- Special RUSH delivery is available. Please call our toll-free phone number for rates.

Save money when you order in quantity

We offer substantial discounts on orders of ten or more copies of any single title. Please call for more information.

Send us your manuscript

Wilder Publishing Center continually seeks manuscripts and proposals for publications in the fields of nonprofit management and community building. Send us your proposal or manuscript. Or, if you'd like more information, call us at 1-800-274-6024 and ask for our Author Guidelines.

Visit our website at www.wilder.org

Order Form
Prices subject to change

	QTY.	PRICE EACH	TOTAL AMOUNT
Collaboration Handbook: Creating, Sustaining, and Enjoying the Journey		$28.00	
Collaboration: What Makes It Work		14.00	
Community Building: What Makes It Work		20.00	
Coping with Cutbacks (working title)		25.00	
Foundations for Violence-Free Living		45.00	
On the Level (participant's workbook to Foundation's for Violence-Free Living)		15.00	
Journey Beyond Abuse (facilitator's guide)		45.00	
Moving Beyond Abuse (participant's journal)		10.00	
The Little Book of Peace (minimum order 10 copies)		0.65	
Marketing Workbook for Nonprofit Organizations Volume I: Develop the Marketing Plan		25.00	
Marketing Workbook for Nonprofit Organizations Volume II: Mobilize People for Marketing Success		25.00	
Pocket Guide for Marketing Representatives		1.95	
Strategic Planning Workbook for Nonprofit Organizations, Revised and Updated		25.00	
What Works in Preventing Rural Violence		17.00	
SUBTOTAL			
In MN, please add 7% sales tax or attach exempt certificate			
SHIPPING			
TOTAL			

Amherst H. Wilder Foundation
Publishing Center
919 Lafond Avenue
St. Paul, MN 55104

Toll-Free 1-800-274-6024
Fax: (612) 642-2061

Name _____

Organization _____

Address _____

_____

City _____ State _____ Zip _____

Phone *(in case we have questions)* (_____) _____

Payment Method: VISA MasterCard AMERICAN EXPRESS Cards

Card # _____

Expiration Date _____

Signature (required) _____

☐ Check/Money Order (payable to A.H. Wilder Foundation)

☐ Bill Me (for orders under $100) Purchase Order # _____